undocumented
and
unafraid

Tam Tran, Cinthya Felix, and the Immigrant Youth Movement

Edited by Kent Wong, Janna Shadduck-Hernández, Fabiola Inzunza,
Julie Monroe, Victor Narro, and Abel Valenzuela Jr.

UCLA Center for Labor Research and Education
Los Angeles, California

"I chose to get arrested because of our politicians' callousness toward a pressing issue that affects not only me but also thousands of other youth on a daily basis. I had the courage, strength, and opportunity to participate in this civil disobedience action thanks to the dedication, valor, and love of others in this movement. Inaction was just not an option for me."
—Diana Yael Martinez *(pictured on front cover)*

Cover photo courtesy of *Washington Post*/Getty Images
Book design by Wendell Pascual

UCLA Center for Labor Research and Education
Los Angeles, CA 90095-1478
© 2012 by UCLA Center for Labor Research and Education
All rights reserved. Published 2012
Printed in the United States of America

Library of Congress Control Number: 2011940899
ISBN 978-0-9836289-3-4

The UCLA Center for Labor Research and Education gratefully acknowledges the generous support of the Ford Foundation toward the publication of this book.

Undocumented and Unafraid beautifully honors Cinthya Felix and Tam Tran by weaving together inspiring details of their lives with the fierce work of the young leaders who are carrying on their legacy. Written largely by the very youth whose futures are at stake, each piece reflects the camaraderie, respect, and dedication that make this one of the greatest civil rights movements of our time.

—Leisy J. Abrego, Assistant Professor, University of California, Los Angeles

Undocumented and Unafraid is a deeply moving book that pays tribute to two courageous young women: Tam Tran and Cinthya Felix. In the face of the unconscionable barriers our broken immigration system placed before them, Tam and Cinthya were Americans through and through, and they embodied the American spirit of fighting for what is right. As a lifelong champion of immigrant rights and the author of the California Dream Act, I am inspired by Tam, Cinthya, and the immigrant youth leaders captured in this book. They are, and forever will be, my heroes.

—Gilbert Cedillo, Assemblymember, State of California

We have raised up a phenomenal generation of children and young people, largely unknown to the mainstream culture, who call themselves "Dream Act" students. Because of the shameful failures of our government, these young people hide from the manufactured hatreds and fears as they finish high school and college, nurturing their lives for God's purposes. Now many of these students audaciously insist that all of us support their humanity. With me, they proclaim, "In the sight of the creator, there are no illegal or undocumented human beings." They are our children. Through them, history writes that we will continue our journey toward equality, liberty, and justice for all.

—Rev. James Lawson Jr., Civil Rights Leader

This book invokes tears, laughter, outrage, and boundless admiration. Entwining the personal and political, the humble and heroic, the trivial and the tragic, the stories of Tam, Cinthya, and their fellow dreamers compel all of us to make our nation what it can and should be.

—Jeannie Oakes, Director of Educational Opportunity and Scholarship, Ford Foundation

Undocumented and Unafraid is a moving tribute to two brilliant and captivating activists, Tam Tran and Cinthya Felix. It is also a powerful call to action to continue their legacy. The book lays out a new canon for youth activism in the twenty-first century that will undoubtedly inspire future generations and cement the immigrant youth movement in its rightful place in American history.

—William Perez, Associate Professor, Claremont Graduate University

Documenting the extraordinary activities and accomplishments of the courageous Dream student activists, these essays are an invaluable record of a critical period in our national history. Like their civil rights predecessors nearly half a century ago and at great risk to themselves and their families, these activists have undertaken to increase understanding of the injustice in our current law and policy through multiple, creative, and effective means. Their efforts, on a trajectory toward ultimate success, are of singular importance in arriving at immigration policies that better reflect our national values and interests.

—Thomas A. Saenz, President and General Counsel, MALDEF

Undocumented and Unafraid captures the powerful stories of courageous young people who are at the forefront of a new civil rights movement in this country. America is a land of immigrants, and immigrant workers helped to organize some of our first unions. The American labor movement stands in solidarity with the immigrant youth movement. Those who are attacking immigrants are also attacking unions. But these young people have learned that when we organize and fight together, we win together.

—Richard Trumka, President, AFL-CIO

Never underestimate the power of the human spirit. That much is clear after reading the stories—unforgettable, inspiring, searing stories—of the people and places documented in this volume.

—Jose Antonio Vargas, Journalist and Founder, Define American

contents

contents

contents

faculty preface

On May 15, 2010, two University of California, Los Angeles (UCLA), alumni and nationally known leaders of the immigrant youth movement, Tam Tran and Cinthya Felix, were tragically killed in a car accident by a drunk driver. This book is dedicated to their memory, to their courage, and to their spirit.

On May 17, 2010, more than five hundred somber students, faculty, and staff gathered together on UCLA's campus for a memorial tribute to Tam and Cinthya, whose tragic deaths have inspired a new generation of activists to carry on the work they left behind.

Also on May 17, four heroic, undocumented students staged a civil disobedience action in the office of Senator John McCain in Phoenix, Arizona. This was the first time in US history that undocumented students voluntarily submitted to arrest, knowing that their actions might result in their deportation and separation from friends and family.

Three days later, nine brave students staged a civil disobedience action in front of the West Los Angeles Federal Building near UCLA, taking over the street and blocking traffic on the heavily traversed Wilshire Boulevard for two full hours.

These events signaled the beginning of nascent protest that blossomed into a national movement.

In the following months, more courageous undocumented students launched other actions, such as the Dream Freedom Ride from Los Angeles to Washington, DC. Others participated in hunger strikes, and still others staged a civil disobedience act in the halls of Congress. These courageous and student-led actions attracted national publicity and generated support from millions of people throughout the country.

With few resources and no paid lobbyists, undocumented immigrant students captured the attention of the president, Congress, and the country, by mobilizing support for the Development, Relief, and Education for Alien Minors (DREAM) Act, which if passed, would provide the opportunity for hundreds of thousands of undocumented immigrant youth to earn legal status by pursuing a college education or serving in the US military. In December 2010, in a historical first, the US House of Representatives passed the DREAM Act, only to

Kent Wong. *Courtesy of Pocho1.*

fail to overcome a filibuster by a minority in the Senate a few weeks later. The euphoria over the act's passage in the House and the disappointment over its failure in the Senate only strengthened the resolve of immigrant students and their supporters. In spite of this setback, the immigrant youth movement came closer than ever to winning passage of the DREAM Act, and the fight continues.

More than two million immigrant youth have been brought to this country as children and for many, this is the only country they have ever known or can remember. Undocumented students are not allowed to apply for driver's licenses in most states, are prohibited from obtaining government financial aid, are barred from access to student loans, and are ineligible for most scholarships. In spite of these barriers, immigrant students are among the most committed and dedicated of their generation. They work very hard in their pursuit of the American dream.

Janna Shadduck-Hernández.

For example, many undocumented immigrant students ride the bus for hours each day to get to school, work long hours in the cash-based economy to support themselves, and in spite of tremendous obstacles, are earning their college degrees and even entering graduate programs. But even with a degree, under the current immigration laws, these college graduates are prohibited from legally working and realizing their full economic and social potential.

Each year, approximately sixty-five thousand undocumented immigrant students graduate from US high schools, twenty-five thousand in California alone. Without the DREAM Act, these young people will forever be relegated to a life in the underground economy—unable to fully contribute to society, participate in the formal workforce, or support the next generation of retirees through our tax system. This current situation harms everyone, especially the students and the US economy.

America is a land of immigrants. We have benefitted from the contributions of immigrants for generations and by all indications, we will continue to reap the benefits from current and future arrivals. The treatment of immigrant youth today is not just mean-spirited; it is un-American and economically foolish. In the face of fierce and contentious debate on immigration policy, youth and students have frequently been ignored or invisible. But silent and invisible no more, undocumented youth are organizing and leading a national movement to create a pathway to their legal normalization.

In 2001, Assembly Bill 540 was signed into law in California, allowing undocumented students to attend public colleges without having to pay out-of-state tuition. This crucial piece of legislation dramatically increased the number of undocumented students attending public colleges in California. In 2011, the California Dream Act, comprised of Assembly Bills 130 and 131, was passed, making California the third state in the nation to offer financial aid to undocumented immigrant students.

In the past ten years, UCLA has benefitted from a large number of brilliant and talented undocumented students who have enrolled and graduated, often overcoming insurmountable odds and difficult

Victor Narro. *Courtesy of Pocho1.*

The UCLA Center for Labor Research and Education has been at the forefront of supporting immigrant students. In 2007, the center taught the very first class on undocumented immigrant students and in 2008 published the first book ever written by and for undocumented immigrant students, *Underground Undergrads: UCLA Undocumented Immigrant Students Speak Out.* The book is currently in its fourth printing and has been used as a textbook in college and high-school classes throughout the country; as an educational resource to advise teachers, parents, and students on the challenges and options facing undocumented students; and as an organizing tool to advocate for the rights of immigrant youth.

Undocumented and Unafraid: Tam Tran, Cinthya Felix, and the Immigrant Youth Movement, like *Underground Undergrads*, was written by and for undocumented immigrant students. It is fitting that the title of the first book captured an earlier stage in the development of this movement, when undocumented students led an underground existence. They were hidden from the public eye, lived their lives in the shadows, and carefully concealed their undocumented status from their classmates and from university administrators, faculty, and staff.

But the campaign has grown and matured, and 2010 marked a major transformation in the US immigrant youth movement. Undocumented students throughout the country have embraced a new slogan, Undocumented and Unafraid. They have realized that their silence was inhibiting their ability to organize and mobilize support for their cause. Although they take risks by speaking out and face the threat of deportation by going public about their immigration status, they face a greater risk by remaining silent. Unless the broken immigration laws of our country are changed, undocumented immigrant students will forever be relegated to a life in hiding, trapped in dead-end, low-paying

circumstances. Were it not for the legal and financial constraints they face, many of these students could attend any college or university of their choosing throughout the country.

Because Los Angeles has one of the largest concentrations of immigrants in the country, UCLA has attracted record numbers of undocumented students over the past ten years. UCLA has also emerged as a focal point for the new immigrant student movement advocating for full rights for undocumented youth. These young people have organized a powerful undocumented student support organization, IDEAS (Improving Dreams, Equality, Access and Success), which has emerged as a model for similar student groups throughout California and across the country. UCLA students have organized teach-ins and public hearings with elected officials, have shared their stories before national media, have testified in the halls of Congress, and have staged rallies, marches, and civil disobedience actions.

jobs, with few opportunities to attend and graduate from college. Those who do graduate will be unable to utilize their degrees because they cannot legally be employed.

Many in the undocumented student movement have come to understand that they have nothing to be ashamed of; indeed, it is members of Congress who should be ashamed for perpetuating unjust laws that marginalize immigrant youth, their families, and communities, and damage our society as a whole. An opportunity to support thousands of young people by rewarding them for attending college or enrolling in the military has been squandered.

As UCLA faculty and educators, we believe it is our duty to stand with our students, to help share their stories, and to challenge unjust immigration laws. UCLA as an institution has been enriched by the presence of undocumented students on our campus, and immigrant students throughout the country have inspired educators everywhere through their perseverance to fulfill their educational dreams.

We will forever be grateful for the opportunity to have Tam Tran and Cinthya Felix as our students, and we will always remember their courage and compassion. Indeed, it is they who taught us. We learned from Tam and Cinthya about the challenges facing undocumented students, the struggles their families and communities endure, and the amazing tenacity and resilience of immigrant youth. Tam's and Cinthya's lives embodied the slogan Undocumented and Unafraid. They were scholars, activists, and leaders. They graduated from UCLA, entered

Ivy League graduate schools, publicly spoke out for immigrant youth, organized for social justice, and maintained their sense of dignity and purpose in the face of daunting obstacles. They remain our heroes.

We dedicate this book to Tam and Cinthya and to the new generation of immigrant youth activists who have emerged from the shadows. These undocumented and unafraid immigrant youth are playing a transformative role within our society and are demanding that our nation of immigrants fulfills its promise to provide liberty and justice for all.

Kent Wong, UCLA Center for Labor Research and Education

Janna Shadduck-Hernández, UCLA Center for Labor Research and Education

Victor Narro, UCLA Center for Labor Research and Education

Abel Valenzuela Jr., UCLA César E. Chávez Department of Chicana/o Studies

student preface

Undocumented and Unafraid: Tam Tran, Cinthya Felix, and the Immigrant Youth Movement is a student publication written in collaboration with faculty and teaching assistants at UCLA. The project grew out of a class offered by the UCLA Center for Labor Research and Education entitled "Immigrant Rights, Labor, and Higher Education" in the fall of 2010. The articles were written by students, educators, and activists from across the country. Their stories provide a written record of the immigrant youth movement.

The student publication team worked on the research, editing, layout, and design. The class included undocumented students and those with legal status, although most of us come from immigrant backgrounds. As undergraduates, we were able to apply our passion to this project through our participation as student editors, bringing the stories in the book to life through images and photography, and above all, by elevating the powerful words of the authors.

The purpose of *Undocumented and Unafraid* is threefold. First, it is a dedication to Tam Tran and Cinthya Felix, two inspiring undocumented women and leaders of the immigrant youth movement, whose unexpected deaths in 2010 were mourned by people nationwide. Second, it captures the voices and experiences of undocumented immigrant youth as the leaders of their struggle. Third, the book includes student research on the day-to-day experiences of undocumented students.

We hope this publication will help to change the opinions, hearts, and minds of people who have misperceptions about undocumented youth. We also hope that it encourages people to answer the call to action and to take a stand with the immigrant youth movement, which has led a powerful campaign to pass the DREAM Act. While undocumented students and their allies have been paving the way for the passage of the DREAM Act since its introduction in Congress in 2001, the immigrant youth movement is much bigger than a single piece of legislation. This movement is about achieving social justice and realizing one of the fundamental principles upon which America was built—equal opportunity for all.

acknowledgments

The UCLA Center for Labor Research and Education would like to first acknowledge the memory and legacy of Tam Tran and Cinthya Felix, whose impact on the immigrant youth movement lives on.

We are grateful to our publication coordinator Fabiola Inzunza, who worked endless hours with the authors, artists, researchers, editors, and the student publication team.

This book grew out of a UCLA course on undocumented immigrant students. The course was designed and taught by faculty from the UCLA Center for Labor Research and Education. The other UCLA departments who sponsored this course were the César E. Chávez Department of Chicana/o Studies, the Asian American Studies Center, and the Institute for Research on Labor and Employment. We would like to thank the teaching associates who were instrumental in supporting the course: Fabiola Inzunza, Cyndi Bendezu, Laura Enriquez, Carlos Amador, David Cho, and Nancy Meza. We would also like acknowledge the interns who were part of the Dream Resource Center and supported the project through its various phases. Thanks to the UCLA César E. Chávez Department of Chicana/o Studies and the Center for the Study of Urban Poverty for their financial support for this publication.

Our sincere thanks to all the students for their hard work, innovative ideas, and contributions, including the editorial team, Helen Yi, Cristina Barrera, Maria Rabinovitch, Maria Penaloza, and Heart Ilaloa. We also thank the authors and family interviewers, Marcos Martinez, Rocio Trujillo, and Thai Le, as well as the photo design and layout team, Diane Velez, Alison Chandler, and May Kim, with the support of Jose Ortiz, Karina Alvarado, and Vanessa Hermoso. We would like to recognize the research team and the authors and interviewers for the research pieces, Edna Monroy, Magali Sanchez-Hall, Abigail Bangalon, Natalie Sheckter, May Kim, Elizabeth Alvarado, Stephanie Camacho, Daniel Cordova, Idalia Lazo, Sammy Medel, Omar Serrano, Margarita Peralta, Claudia Grajeda, Tania Mendoza, Sean Perez, and Gerardo Vindiola.

Immigrant youth organizations whose members contributed to this publication in various capacities include Improving Dreams, Equality, Access, and Success at UCLA; Dream Team Los Angeles; the Queer Undocumented Youth Collective; Orange County Dream Team; Brown Immigrant Rights Coalition; Student Immigrant Movement; Trail of Dreams; North Carolina Dream Team; Asian Students Promoting Immigrant Rights through Education; Dreamers Adrift; National Immigrant Youth Alliance; Dreamactivist.org; and United We Dream. We are honored to feature Diana Yael Martinez on the cover, a courageous dreamer who was arrested during a civil disobedience action at the US capitol.

acknowledgments

We would like to thank the following authors who contributed to this publication: the Felix family, the Tran family, Dana Heatherton, Susan Melgarejo, Fabiola Inzunza, Deana Duran, Jeff Cooper, Nancy Mejia, Tom Osborne, Stephanie Solis, Matthew Garcia, Angela Chen, Tracy Buenavista, Gaby Pacheco, Renata Teodoro, Matias Ramos, Ireri Unzueta, Lizbeth Mateo, Mohammad Abdollahi, Tania Unzueta, Yahaira Carrillo, Raúl Alcaraz, Nancy Meza, Cyndi Bendezu, Laura Lopez, Maricela Aguilar, Carlos Amador, Cristina Jimenez, David Cho, Prerna Lal, Flavia de la Fuente, Imelda Plascencia, Jorge Gutierrez, Catherine Eusebio, Abigail Bangalon, Margarita Peralta, Laura Enriquez, Edna Monroy, Natalie Sheckter, Nancy Guarneros, and Citlalli Chavez.

We would also like to thank the following photographers and artists for their contributions: Nery Orellana, Erick Huerta, Peter Holderness, Raymundo M. Hernández-López, Anselmo Rascon, Jonathan Bibriesca, Xavi Moreno, Remeike Forbes, Julio Salgado, Adrian Gonzalez, Maria Rabinovitch, Justin Valas, Pocho1, and Freddy Pech. The following individuals also contributed photography: Dana Heatherton, Susan Melgarejo, Stephanie Solis, Eric Yao, Josh Savala, Angela Chen, Horacio Arroyo, Sophia Sandoval, Patricia Torres, Cyndi Bendezu, Fabiola Inzunza, Matias Ramos, and Nancy Meza.

Special thanks go to our talented book designer Wendell Pascual.

Student editors in the Immigrant Rights, Labor, and Higher Education course, fall 2010.
Courtesy of Maria Rabinovitch.

Part I

the lives of tam tran
and cinthya felix

SUPPORT THE DREAM ACT

Nery Orellana, 2010

At a time when saying

"I am undocumented"

was a radical statement,
they said it with **pride**

—IDEAS (Improving Dreams, Equality, Access and Success) at UCLA

Tam Tran and Cinthya Felix were trailblazers. As early leaders of the immigrant youth movement, they were among this generation's first group of undocumented students to graduate from college and enter graduate school. Against all odds, they were models of success. The following articles offer a unique view into their short but meaningful lives as daughters, sisters, friends, activists, and scholars. These are reflections from those who knew Tam and Cinthya best.

introduction:
tam tran and cinthya felix
undocumented and unafraid

Kent Wong and Matias Ramos

Cinthya and Tam in Central Park, 2009.
Courtesy of the Felix family.

On May 15, 2010, Tam Tran and Cinthya Felix, leaders in the movement to pass the DREAM Act, were killed in a car accident. Their tragic passing has galvanized the movement they left behind.

The Development, Relief, and Education for Alien Minors (DREAM) Act proposes to grant United States citizenship to undocumented students or those who entered the country as children. It was first introduced in Congress in 2001 under a different name and has been reintroduced several times, most recently in 2010. The effort to get the bill enacted into law has been growing for a decade, and the national campaign for its passage has emerged as one of the most important social-justice movements of this generation. Students who stand to benefit from the law have conducted civil disobedience in the halls of Congress; organized hunger strikes; marched in the Trail of Dreams from Florida to Washington, DC;

orchestrated the Dream Freedom Ride from Los Angeles to Washington, DC; and participated in many other actions.

The movement to pass the DREAM Act arose in the hearts and minds of thousands of young immigrants who claim America as their home; the movement has created powerful bonds among these young activists who are assuming leadership roles and shaping the nation's future.

Tam and Cinthya both grew up in undocumented immigrant families. Against the odds, both graduated from the University of California, Los Angeles (UCLA) and entered prestigious graduate schools. Indeed, Tam and Cinthya were among the very few undocumented immigrant graduate students in the country. Tam was enrolled in a doctoral program in American civilization at Brown University; Cinthya was in a master's program in public health at Columbia University, and she planned to apply for medical school. Both were leading advocates for passage of the DREAM Act, both with a national reputation as activists. Dream students are carrying on Tam's and Cinthya's work in their honor and memory.

Of the estimated eleven million undocumented immigrants currently living in the United States, more than two million are minors. These young people had no say in the decision to come to this country; they were brought here by parents or relatives seeking a better life. The aim of the DREAM Act is to give those young people an opportunity to earn legal status by completing two years of higher education or through service in the US military.

Dream activists like Tam and Cinthya became advocates for their own legal status as part of the broader fight for immigration reform. The rise in visibility of such activists challenged the pejorative labels of "illegal" and "law-breaking" frequently used in congressional and media debates on immigration. Tam and Cinthya and others like them showed America a different, more accurate image of undocumented youth that exemplified all that we value and hope for in our children: leadership, courage, articulateness, civic-minded commitment, and professional skills. They epitomized the motto of the DREAM Act movement: Undocumented and Unafraid. Breaking the habit of fear and anonymity by sharing their stories, they advanced a powerful movement for social justice.

When Tam was six years old, the Tran family came to the United States to join other family members who had settled in California. Tam's parents applied for political asylum, but their request was denied after many years because they had emigrated from Germany rather than directly from Vietnam. The family received a withholding of deportation exemption, but their status provides no path to legal residency or US citizenship. Tam was Vietnamese, but she had never been to Vietnam and was not a Vietnamese citizen. She was born in Germany, but Germany does not grant citizenship based on birthright. And although Tam spent more than twenty years in the United States, the American government refused to grant her legal status. So she was not only undocumented but also stateless, trapped in a disgraceful immigration morass.

Tam grew up in Garden Grove, California. She graduated from Santiago High School, attended Santa Ana College, and then transferred to UCLA. She worked multiple jobs while carrying a full course load and was also a prominent student leader and activist. At UCLA, she found a home with IDEAS, the support organization for undocumented immigrant students. She was a gifted filmmaker who produced acclaimed documentaries that have been screened nationwide. The two best-known are *Lost and Found* and *The Seattle Underground Railroad* (2007). Both capture the stories of undocumented UCLA students and celebrate the struggles and accomplishments of young immigrants. These moving, humorous, and insightful films provide a sharp analysis of oppressive immigration laws and their impact on youth.

Tam gave public talks on the DREAM Act, screened her films, and promoted *Underground Undergrads*, the UCLA Labor

Tam, Cinthya, and fellow UCLA alumna Marla Ramirez at an immigrant rights rally in Washington, DC, 2010. *Courtesy of the Felix family.*

Center student publication on undocumented immigrant students, throughout the country. She made presentations before the national convention of the Asian Pacific American Labor Alliance in Nevada, to the first Asian Pacific worker rights hearing in Washington, DC, and at the 2009 American Sociological Association conference in San Francisco, to name a few. Each time, she spoke with eloquence, grace, and power, and each time, she recruited more allies to support the movement of immigrant youth and students.

As a leading national advocate for the DREAM Act, Tam testified before the US Congressional Immigration Subcommittee on May 18, 2007. Given her undocumented status, this was an act of considerable personal courage. Three days later, ICE (Immigration and Customs Enforcement) agents staged a predawn raid on her family's home in Orange County and took her parents and brother into custody. Tam reached out to members of Congress and immigration attorneys and succeeded in getting her family released and stopping their deportation. Throughout this ordeal, she kept her focus, remarking, "My family is one of the lucky ones. Most immigrants don't have access to Congress and immigration attorneys; they just disappear."

Tam entered the doctoral program in American civilization at Brown University. She joked, "Maybe if I get a PhD in American civilization, they will finally let me become an American." In Rhode Island as in California, she swiftly became a leader. She continued to advocate for passage of the DREAM Act, founded the Brown Immigrant Rights Coalition (BIRC), and helped launch the first statewide network of undocumented immigrant youths and students. She mobilized student contingents for marches in Washington, DC, and lobbying visits to the Rhode Island congressional delegation and statehouse. A few weeks after her death, Brown University awarded her a master's degree in recognition of her extraordinary achievements.

Tam and Cinthya in New York, 2010. *Courtesy of the Felix family.*

Cinthya Felix was born in Sinaloa, Mexico, on January 23, 1984. At fifteen, her parents moved the family to Los Angeles in an attempt to survive economically. The Felix family settled in the historic Mexican community of East Los Angeles. In high school, Cinthya was a brilliant student and an accomplished basketball player. She enrolled at UCLA, a two-hour commute by bus. She worked hard, saved money, and bought a car, audaciously giving it the vanity license plate YLLEGAL.

Like other undocumented immigrants, Cinthya was unable to get a driver's license in California. She understood the contradiction: "The state wants our money, so they let us buy the car, get insurance, and pay for registration. But when it comes to giving us a license, they don't want to give you one" (Tran 2007). She could not get a license in California, but she had a plan. She organized a group of students to drive to the state of Washington, where it is easier for immigrants to obtain driver's licenses. Tam Tran was one of the few students in IDEAS who had a driver's license, so she joined the trip and brought her camera to document the experience, producing the film *The Seattle Underground Railroad*.

At UCLA, Cinthya was one of the founders of IDEAS, which began as a clandestine support group. Undocumented students gathered to share survival tips and assist one another in navigating the frequently unfriendly waters of the big university. As the group's numbers grew, it developed into a bold public-advocacy organization, orchestrating mock graduation ceremonies on campus, immigrant youth empowerment conferences that drew hundreds of students to UCLA, and an annual banquet that raised funds for members to complete their educations. Cinthya and Tam became leading activists and fast friends. After their deaths, IDEAS was recognized by the University of California's president and regents as an outstanding student organization within the university.

Cinthya graduated with a degree in English literature and minors in Spanish and Mexican studies, but her ambition was to have a career in medicine. Since she was certain that medical schools would not accept applicants without legal status, she decided to apply to master's degree programs in public health instead, eventually choosing Columbia University. In graduate school, she conducted research on health care access within immigrant communities, while waiting tables at night to support herself.

Tam and Cinthya were pioneers, undocumented immigrant students who had made it into graduate programs at exclusive private universities. But this achievement was not without its share of alienation and isolation. As they had in California, Tam and Cinthya relied on each other, and their experiences on the East Coast only deepened their friendship. To celebrate the end of the school year, they took a road trip to Maine to visit lighthouses, eat lobster, and prepare for summer. As they were returning from their trip, they were killed by a drunk driver who swerved into their lane of traffic.

Two days later, more than five hundred students gathered at UCLA for a memorial in Tam's and Cinthya's honor. Vigils were held in Los Angeles, Orange County, New York, Washington, DC, Rhode Island, and Florida. Students in Arizona made buttons bearing Tam's and Cinthya's pictures. Most importantly, students in many areas of the country commemorated Tam's and Cinthya's spirit by carrying on their work, staging sit-ins, street closures, civil disobedience actions, hunger strikes, the Dream Freedom Ride, and other activities. These untimely deaths have been mourned and memorialized by members of Congress, the California state legislature, the Los Angeles County Board of Supervisors, and the Los Angeles City Council. In Tam's and Cinthya's memory, Dream activists reaffirmed their commitment to fight for the DREAM Act.

Although we mourn the passing of Cinthya and Tam, we celebrate their lives. They were sisters; they were kindred spirits, always in sync, planning their next meal, their next act of defiant and optimistic activism, searching for a new adventure, pursuing their next dream. They accomplished more in their short lives than ever could have been imagined. Their spirit lives on in the hundreds of IDEAS alumni, in the thousands of young immigrants who embrace them as role models, and in the millions of immigrants who will one day be empowered to emerge from the shadows.

Reference

Tran, Tam. 2007. *The Seattle Underground Railroad.*

Originally published in an edited form in *Boom: A Journal of California* 1 (1). http://www.boomcalifornia .com/2011/03/undocumented-and-unafraid-tam-tran-and-cinthya-felix/.

A Step toward Accessing Higher Education in California: Assembly Bill 540

Undocumented students generally do not qualify for state or federal financial aid, and many live in low-income households. California Assembly Bill 540 (AB 540) lifts one of the many barriers that immigrant youth encounter upon entering higher education.

With the passage of AB 540 in October 2001, California became the second state, after Texas, in the United States to offer in-state tuition to undocumented youth. The bill was authored by the late Assemblymember Marco A. Firebaugh, majority floor leader and chair of the California Latino Legislative Caucus. Firebaugh's work has inspired many in California to continue fighting for access to higher education through other initiatives, such as the California Dream Act, which allows AB 540-eligible students to access financial aid.

In order to qualify for AB 540, students must have attended a California high school for at least three years, have earned a California high-school diploma or passed the General Educational Development (GED) tests, and upon enrolling in a public California university or college, sign an affidavit affirming qualification for in-state tuition. If undocumented, students must declare that they intend to adjust their status as soon as they are eligible to do so.

While some undocumented students are able to qualify for in-state tuition under AB 540, permanent residents and US citizens form the majority of beneficiaries. For instance, AB 540 grants in-state tuition to previous California residents who return to the state to attend college, until they are able to declare California residency again. Even though the bill primarily assists the education of native students, the law has been challenged in the California courts. The *Martinez v. Regents* lawsuit was filed in 2005 by out-of-state students and interest groups who sought to repeal the law because it helps undocumented students. In October 2010, the California Supreme Court upheld the law.

AB 540 has also evolved into an identity marker for many undocumented youth in California. Some undocumented students self-identify as "AB 540 students" and have used the term interchangeably with "undocumented students" to distinguish themselves and their unique struggles.

UCLA IDEAS members welcome incoming AB 540 students, 2011. *Courtesy of IDEAS at UCLA.*

Supporting Our Dreams: IDEAS at UCLA

Improving Dreams, Equality, Access and Success (IDEAS) is a support and advocacy group for undocumented students at UCLA. Students, staff, faculty, and administrators came together and officially established the organization in October 2003.

Completely run by undocumented students at UCLA, IDEAS hosts dozens of workshops and conferences throughout the year, targeting local communities, school counselors, and educators who request information about how to better serve their undocumented youth populations. The annual Immigrant Youth Empowerment Conference is attended by over a thousand potential college students who learn from each other about the resources available to them after high school.

IDEAS also focuses on fund-raising for scholarships to help keep undocumented students in school. With rising tuition costs and with no financial aid available to them, IDEAS has been able to coordinate a scholarship program for their members since 2005. This scholarship, while small, has helped a number of IDEAS members stay in school and stay active within the organization.

As an advocacy group, IDEAS has consistently taken an active role at the campus, regional, state, and national levels, to campaign for equal access to higher education for all students, regardless of their immigration status. They continue to build strong alliances with community members, as they join forces to fight for their dreams.

Over a thousand students from all over California register for the fourth annual Immigrant Youth Empowerment Conference at UCLA, 2011. *Courtesy of IDEAS at UCLA.*

sisters in the movement

Fabiola Inzunza

I first met Cinthya Felix during my senior year in high school. I had been accepted to UCLA and was invited to the campus to learn what to expect as an undergraduate. Cinthya was learning how to drive when she picked me up in her dusty Jeep. I had recently learned that being undocumented meant that even though I had been accepted to a prestigious university, I would not be eligible for financial aid or other university resources to finance my education.

When we arrived at UCLA, Cinthya walked me to the administration building and advised me to fill out several forms that would allow me to pay in-state tuition. The bill that made this possible, AB 540, had just been passed through the California legislature three years earlier, and Cinthya was among the first wave of undocumented college students to benefit from it. This bill made it possible for me to even imagine being able to pay for college.

Then Cinthya walked me over to my first IDEAS meeting, a group that had formed a few months earlier as a support organization for undocumented students at UCLA. I met many other undocumented students who were somehow surviving. I thought if they could do it, I had the strength to continue as well.

After the IDEAS meeting, Cinthya walked me to another building, where I met Jeff Cooper from the Academic Advancement Project. He helped me fill out other forms to enroll in a summer program that would assist me with the transition to the university. This program cemented the bond I had with UCLA and pushed me to survive and persevere for the next six years of my life. The few hours Cinthya spent showing me around the campus opened doors to a lifetime of opportunities for me.

I quickly got involved with IDEAS and met Tam Tran. She had also just started at UCLA, but she had come in as a transfer student from community college. Tam became the first IDEAS historian, documenting every meeting and event with her handheld video camera. I went on to become membership chair, which allowed me to work with IDEAS members to address the needs of undocumented students on campus. Cinthya helped to launch some of our first fund-raising efforts toward a scholarship for undocumented students at UCLA.

The few hours Cinthya spent
showing me around the campus
opened doors to a
lifetime of opportunities
for me

Tam, *second from right*, and Cinthya, *fourth from right*, with IDEAS members and allies, winter 2005. *Courtesy of IDEAS at UCLA.*

IDEAS grew exponentially with new members contributing their creativity and talent. With limited resources, IDEAS became a powerful institution of its own. We also became a family.

During finals week one quarter, we learned that a fellow member's father had been deported. ICE agents had come to his home early one morning looking for someone else. But because her father had no identification card, ICE took him instead. Our friend did not return to her home for fear of being deported, and she was left with no place to live. She had just finished paying for tuition at UCLA, and she had no money left. Without hesitation, Tam invited her to move in, and she lived with Tam for

several months. This is the type of caring friend that Tam was to so many.

Cinthya and Tam were our sisters, and they were the first people I organized with in the struggle for immigrant rights. They were among the first to embody the fierce slogan of our movement, Undocumented and Unafraid.

It has been an honor to serve as one of the editors of this book. I was devastated by Tam's and Cinthya's passing, and working on this book has been a healing process for me. I am so proud to be able to help preserve their legacy and to work with such amazing immigrant youth activists across the country who are carrying on Tam's and Cinthya's spirit.

not your typical activists

Dana Heatherton

Tam Tran didn't carry a bullhorn or lead chants at rallies. She wasn't a shopaholic, but she shopped without guilt. She kept a stack of unworn clothes next to her bed and bought fancy cameras and funny socks. Tam loved technology, punk rock, asymmetrical haircuts, and fried food. Tam was such a great activist because she was easy to relate to. That is why she inspired everyone around her.

I met Tam as we were handing in our applications for the McNair Research Scholars Program at UCLA. She didn't say a word to me even as we left together, hopped on the same empty bus, and exited at the same stop. We were neighbors, interested in similar research, and wearing almost identical outfits. It was clear we had much in common, but we didn't speak. It wasn't until later that I learned Tam was undocumented and didn't know who she could trust. She seemed quiet and reserved, but she wasn't shy. If someone encouraged her to take food home after a meeting, she wouldn't just take a slice of pizza, she would grab the whole box. At our first academic conference, I saw her pile several box lunches in a stack higher than her head and leave, never looking back. I knew at that moment she would be my friend.

I became a regular member of IDEAS at UCLA because of Tam. It was a big deal when Tam joined the group, because she was the first member who was not of Latin American descent. An even bigger deal was when Tam started bringing me to meetings. I was one of the first US-citizen student allies to become a member of IDEAS, and this was understandably a new and scary thing for people. Some joked that I must work for ICE because why would I want to spend my Fridays talking about immigration if I weren't working undercover? But Tam made us learn from each other in the most casual way. I became a part of the movement, and I didn't even realize it.

Though Tam was reserved, she was never afraid to speak up about things she was passionate about. In one thoughtfully argued academic paper, she decided to throw in curse words to emphasize her point. Her refrigerator proudly displayed the D she had earned for using foul language. Tam liked to go against the grain, maybe because she felt most comfortable doing so. Or maybe it was because she had no other choice. When she filled out scholarship applications that asked her to identify her citizenship, she wrote in "Citizen of the World."

But even when she was doing more traditional lobbying and activism in Sacramento or Washington, DC, Tam always minimized the importance of her efforts. When I e-mailed her asking how her trip to Sacramento was going, she responded, "We had IHOP at 50 percent off." One night Tam called asking if I were busy. "Hey, I'm speaking in front of Congress tomorrow. Can you look over my speech?" Tam understated everything. This is what made her cool, but it also made it difficult to understand all that she went through. She told me she cried every year she applied for a work permit and got rejected. But that was the extent of her emotion. There was a lot

OREGON SHAKESPEARE FESTIVAL

ELIZABETHAN

ANGUS BOWMER

NEW THEA

Tam, Cinthya, and Dana on their way to Seattle, 2006. *Courtesy of Dana Heatherton.*

in her life that she could be sad about, but she chose to focus on what made her happy. There were certain things about our backgrounds that we could never fully understand about each other, but we had a special connection that transcended our differences. My problems were her concerns, her accomplishments my joys. We helped each other grow without envy or conceit. Never again will I have a friend to whom I feel so connected. Tam Tran is the best friend I ever had. I miss her every day.

Cinthya Felix was the hardest-working person I knew, always in survival mode. It seemed like she never relaxed. Like most undocumented students, Cinthya had to worry about getting good grades, paying for school, and supporting her family. But Cinthya also made having fun equally important. She worked at it as hard as her other responsibilities, and she always excelled in everything.

Cinthya was organized and always prepared. She was also brilliant. She could figure out every loophole in the system, and she documented it all. Because of her thorough research and organization, hundreds of undocumented high-school students in California have been able to go to college. Cinthya knew which boxes to fill out, which to leave blank, and how to successfully navigate the higher education system before many even knew it was possible. She and other IDEAS members took all the research Cinthya had done for herself and made it available to undocumented parents, educators, and college counselors, so they could learn from her experience. She was a trailblazer.

Cinthya was a role model for her family and the community of East Los Angeles. As busy as she was, Cinthya made time to return to her alma mater, Garfield High School, to speak on panels and encourage kids to go to college. Her younger brothers and sister looked up to her for guidance and hope. Cinthya carried much responsibility because her accomplishments were shared by her whole community, putting a lot of pressure on her not to fail. While people may know that Cinthya carried this weight during her life, many do not know that there was one place where she never had to worry, a place where our friendship grew the most: the basketball court.

On the court, Cinthya could just do what she loved to do. Her shot was relaxed and smooth, and she could run up and down the court with ease. It was the one place where it didn't seem like she had to try hard. She was a good ball handler and a solid three-point shooter. She was a star player in high school and recruited by many colleges. When she came back to Los Angeles for breaks, she spent a lot of time organizing basketball games. Cinthya just loved the game, and I'm grateful that basketball made our friendship stronger.

There was something else unique about our relationship to the game. Cinthya and I both grew up in the Japanese American basketball leagues in Los Angeles as two of the most unlikely people to be seen there. With my red hair and freckles, I was routinely pulled off the court and questioned about my eligibility to play, because I didn't look Japanese enough. Cinthya, on the sidelines, was one of the few non-Asians there, keeping time and tracking stats for the books. We met when she was working part-time as scorekeeper, one of the many jobs she held to put herself through school.

Of course when the games ended, life always came rushing back in. When Cinthya got into the Columbia School of Public Health master's program, she faced one of her greatest challenges. Disqualified for financial aid because of her immigration status, she had to come up with the tuition out-of-pocket. She deferred school for a year to earn enough money. After the year was up, she left for New York City. Once she found a place to live, I flew out to help her

move in. Of course when I got there, she was already unpacked and organized. In no time, she had a great group of friends in the city. But her struggle was far from over. Cinthya still had to work two jobs to support herself. It always saddened me that she couldn't just be a student like everyone else.

To me, Tam and Cinthya were just my friends. I didn't have a sense of their impact. I knew they were incredible people, but I was shocked to see how many lives they touched. I had always thought that leaders and activists were the loudest and the center of attention. But that did not describe my friends. Tam and Cinthya led through example. They gave people hope that you can go to the best schools, stay active within the immigrant rights movement, and still shop compulsively, love music, eat ribs, and play basketball. If you didn't know their immigration status, you wouldn't think twice about it. Sometimes I forgot the burden they always carried.

Memorials for Tam and Cinthya were held across the country for months following their deaths. From Rhode Island to Florida to Washington, DC, people celebrated their lives. From Tam and Cinthya, I learned what real impact means—not how many people mourn your death but how many people learn to act from your life. I am proud to call them my friends.

From Tam and Cinthya, I learned **what real impact means—** not how many people mourn your death but how many people learn to **act from your life**

the last time i saw tam and cinthya

Susan Melgarejo

Tam and Cinthya were my best friends in the whole world. We had many friends and acquaintances, but no one understood us as well as we understood one another. It was the kind of sisterhood that came from sharing the same struggle; we understood each other's fears and worries better than anyone else. We also shared the same approach to life, always striving for success while making sure we took the time to enjoy ourselves.

The last time I saw Tam and Cinthya was on a trip to New York City. They had no problem convincing me to visit the East Coast in the spring of 2010. We had discussed our desire to travel together as much as possible and had agreed to take a trip at least once a year for the rest of our lives. Cinthya and I had visited Las Vegas for New Year's Eve the winter before. We planned a trip with Tam to Yosemite for early summer and to Hawaii for late summer. But our

Susan, Tam, and Cinthya in Central Park, March 2010.
Courtesy of Susan Melgarejo.

dream was to go on a trip around the world after the DREAM Act passed. Professor Tam would leave whichever class she was teaching; Cinthya would take a leave of absence from wherever she was working. We would drop whatever we were doing, max out our credit cards, and leave to look for a new adventure. Both Cinthya and Tam had a future filled with limitless possibilities, for they were adventurous and brave.

As the date arrived for my visit to New York, I wasn't too excited about the trip—I was tired from long workdays and other responsibilities in Los Angeles. But all that went away as soon as I arrived at Cinthya's apartment in New York City, where she was living while attending Columbia University. She received me in her pajamas and gave me a big hug. Cinthya had a way of motivating people and building enthusiasm. I was suddenly excited to see my friend again and explore the city. I knew that I would have great stories to tell with Cinthya as my tour guide—she always had amazing pictures and stories from her travels. Against many people's advice, she once went to Puerto Rico, a US territory that most undocumented students wouldn't visit, given the uncertainty and misconceptions about what kind of documents are needed to fly there and back. Cinthya also went sky diving in San Diego and was able to see the US-Mexico border while jumping off the plane. She joked about how she tried to avoid landing on the Mexican side of the border, which could have effectively resulted in her self-deportation. She never let her immigration status interfere with her sense of freedom.

Tam wasn't scheduled to arrive in New York until that night, so Cinthya took me sight-seeing while she ran errands. She lived a very organized life; she was clean and planned everything, like the character of Monica from the television show *Friends.* Cinthya was always on the go. She was a fast walker and wasted no time. For instance, that day we went to the Brooklyn Bridge, Greenwich Village, and Chelsea Market, and she still worked a full shift at her job. When Tam arrived, we stayed in, and Cinthya threw a wine and cheese party.

The next day, Cinthya had an itinerary for us. We stopped to do some shopping first—shopping was also a big part of their

Saturday morning, we joined a fund-raising rally for the Trail of Dreams. Cinthya was ecstatic about walking to New Jersey, and Tam was enthused to meet up with other activists. Our vacation blended perfectly with our passion and activism.

The Statue of Liberty was scheduled for our last day; Cinthya had bought tickets in advance. Although she wasn't excited about going to see the Statue of Liberty again, she knew that it was important to me. Cinthya had also made brunch reservations at her favorite Cuban restaurant, and Tam was excited about the food. After eating, we took a nap in Central Park. That was the last time all three of us were together.

In their short lives, Tam and Cinthya **experienced more** than most people do in a lifetime

lives. Cinthya had a relaxed style but always kept up with the latest trends, while Tam's style was less trendy and a little bit hipster. I believe Tam's fashion sense was more of an art form than anything materialistic or status seeking. She was often voted "most fashionable" during campus and organization mock awards, and friends often said, "I bought this because I thought it was something Tam would wear."

After shopping, we visited Madison Square Garden, Radio City Music Hall, the Museum of Modern Art, Central Park, and Little Italy. We also reunited with friends from California who now live in New York, meeting people in Times Square, Chinatown, and Brooklyn. Both Cinthya and Tam were skilled at making and keeping friends. Cinthya was always appreciative of people who helped her, and she taught me about thank you cards. Tam was well respected, and people enjoyed her company.

Even though this trip was a planned vacation, the DREAM Act was a daily concern and a big part of our lives. On

Cinthya took a train to work, while Tam and I shopped for souvenirs and did more sight-seeing. Tam had to take a bus back to Rhode Island. The last time I saw Tam, she was leaving the apartment and said to me, "See you later, dude," with a hug. The last time I saw Cinthya, she was asleep. It was four o'clock in the morning, and my flight was leaving. I poked her, "I'm leaving;" she mumbled, "Okay, go." That was the end of our trip.

I had no idea I wasn't going to see my friends again. But if I could go back, I wouldn't change a thing. Their personalities made the trip perfect. In their short lives, Tam and Cinthya experienced more than most people do in a lifetime. They knew how to live life to the fullest, and they shared that with everybody they knew. I learned so much from them that to this day, I take the risks and leaps of faith they would have taken. I learned to make my own path and follow my dreams without hesitation. I'll always treasure the moments we shared together.

my fearless daughter

Irene Perez
Translated and edited by Rocio Trujillo

Our lives changed when we took a vacation to Los Angeles to visit relatives. During our trip, we were invited to watch Cinthya's cousin Jessica play basketball at Garfield High School. Cinthya began to dream about attending and playing basketball for that school and as always, she had already captured the attention of the basketball coach and faculty. Sometime after that trip, my husband lost his job. Realizing that we needed better jobs to support our family, we made a collective decision to move to Los Angeles.

My daughter Cinthya was very distinctive; she was not only energetic and funny but also mature and focused. Although we had only lived in Los Angeles for a few years, by Cinthya's senior year, she had already mastered the steps needed to accomplish her goals. It did not surprise me when she was accepted into many great universities because to Cinthya, there were no limits. One day she came home from school and said, "Mom, I got accepted to this school, and I don't know how I am going to do it, but I am going to go."

Cinthya decided to go to UCLA. She did her best to include our family in the next stage of her life, bringing us to an event for incoming students. During her undergraduate years, my daughter remained a remarkable student. Cinthya wanted to be a doctor, but her immigration status prevented her from pursuing that dream. Consequently, she decided to apply to graduate school, and she got accepted to Columbia University in New York. I asked her how she was going to afford living in New York and as always, she told me, "Mom, don't worry about it. I'm going to go, and I'll figure it out." And so she left without having a place to live, without knowing anybody. I was worried; what was my daughter going to do in a big city like New York? But I let her go. I believed in her as I always had. If my daughter had wanted to go to the moon, she would have found a way to do it.

When Cinthya arrived in New York, she found a place to stay, an apartment with

Cinthya with her mother, 1994. *Courtesy of the Felix family.*

two girls who were also UCLA graduates. She found two jobs, one through school and another at a pizzeria. Her schedule was tough, allowing her to attend school only part-time. I worried at times, but as soon as I got a call and heard how happy she was, I felt at ease. I knew she was fine. One day she told me, "Mom, when I finish school, I'm not going back to Los Angeles, because I see that here there are more opportunities for work." She wanted to be a doctor serving low-income, non-English-speaking communities, because of the poor quality of medical services provided to them. She said that the language barrier allows for misunderstandings that can affect the health of patients, such as doctors' prescribing the wrong medications.

Cinthya had a strong, positive personality. Her determination always amazed me, because she was always one step ahead. I was delighted with my daughter's attitude toward life; I never saw her concerned about the obstacles she faced, although I have to admit her determination scared me at times. I wanted to protect her from getting hurt, in case plans did not turn out the way she pictured them. I just never wanted her to think of herself as a failure. Cinthya was not the type of daughter who depended on us. On the contrary, she would help us, even if she had to sacrifice herself. She always kept her brothers and sister in mind and tried to teach them the things she learned.

Cinthya trusted us and shared both her happy and sad experiences with us. Knowing that we had a good relationship comforts

Cinthya with her parents at her UCLA graduation ceremony, 2007. *Courtesy of the Felix family.*

me in the middle of all this sadness. If my words are of any value to parents out there, I want to say that maintaining good communication with our children is critical. Do not lose a single minute with your children, especially when they share anything about their lives.

Cinthya touched many people's lives. I had never seen the magnitude of her influence until her UCLA memorial. Dozens of people—young, old, and professionals alike—spoke about how she had impacted their lives. I want to tell those people who supported my daughter how grateful we are on her behalf. Thank you for being such an important part of my daughter's life.

If my daughter had wanted to **go to the moon**, she would have **found a way** to do it

my sister cinthya

Nayelli Felix

Edited by Marcos Martinez

Cinthya was a model student in Mexico and through hard work, she demonstrated that she could be an exceptional student in the United States as well. Cinthya was the first in our family to learn English and within a few months, she was taken out of ESL (English as a Second Language) classes. She began taking advanced placement classes and excelled academically with a 4.0 grade point average, graduating fifth in her high-school class.

As Cinthya's English proficiency grew, she became more active in school by joining clubs and participating in extracurricular

Cinthya and Nayelli at Multnomah Falls, Oregon, 2009.
Courtesy of the Felix family.

activities. She was committed to giving back to her community and to those in need. She stayed active in our community by forming a recreational basketball team that my friends and I participated in. While at UCLA, Cinthya's views changed after she learned something could be done to change a person's immigration status. She became involved in immigration rights groups and transformed herself into an advocate for the DREAM Act.

Cinthya was constantly pressuring us to attend marches and rallies, but we seldom went. The trend continued with our extended family, some of whom had the freedom to vote but generally chose not to. These things were upsetting to Cinthya, but nothing upset her more than students who had the advantage of being born here but took their education for granted. She considered these students privileged because they have access to more resources than we do, yet many of them opt to disregard a higher education or drop out of high school.

Cinthya always took me everywhere she went. I felt that she did it because she wanted to prepare me for all of the obstacles she knew I would be facing. We went to AB 540 events and to other happenings that were relevant to our struggle. Unfortunately there were people who only had negative things to say about her aspirations. Some of her teachers and family members discouraged her from dreaming big, telling her that she would not make it far without a social security number. Fortunately for Cinthya, these comments did nothing but increase her drive and encourage her even more.

Much like everything else she did, Cinthya's career choice reflected her kindness and willingness to help others. After graduating from UCLA, she dreamt of becoming a doctor but was barred from medical school for not being a documented resident. Instead of giving up on her dreams, she sought an alternative to medical school, which resulted in her pursuit of a master's degree in public health at Columbia University. Unfortunately Columbia came at an even higher price than UCLA, and she was forced to defer enrollment for a year in order to save money.

Cinthya funded her graduate studies by working as the director of a program at a youth center to assist high school students with math, English, and college applications. Using a grant from a local school

that being undocumented did not mean that we were sentenced to a life without any upward mobility.

I was closest to Cinthya and out of all our siblings, I felt that she was the closest to me. During high school, she always pressured me to work harder; she wanted me to be better than she was. I followed in her footsteps most of my life. When it was time to apply to universities, Cinthya was there as expected. Days before the deadline, I was still working on my personal statement, and I was having a difficult time writing it. Cinthya stayed up with me that night to make sure that I finished. Her suggestions were crucial for my acceptance into the University of California, Santa Barbara.

After submitting my personal statement, I began to lose hope. I had no idea how I

she would tell me she dreamt of one day **becoming a doctor**, buying a house for our parents, and moving them out of our **cramped apartment**

district, she built the program from the ground up. Cinthya was feeling frustrated about the fact that she had worked so hard for her bachelor's degree but could not use it to earn a living. With added stress from work, she was beginning to get discouraged, thinking she was not going to be able to save enough money to go to New York.

The prospect of getting her master's from Columbia motivated Cinthya to work toward her goals, but her main priority was always to help our parents. She saw how hard they worked to make ends meet, often doing jobs that others refused to do. We spoke at length about this issue, and she would tell me she dreamt of one day becoming a doctor, buying a house for our parents, and moving them out of our cramped apartment. Cinthya also worked hard to become a role model. She wanted to show people

was going to pay for school. Once again, Cinthya was there to rescue me. She could not help me with money but instead used her resources to find stacks of scholarship applications. She followed me throughout the application process. It was like having my personal teacher at home. When my orientation date came around, she drove me to Santa Barbara and played my parents' role. There I was faced with many intimidating documents to fill out; some asked for my social security number and other forms of identification to verify my citizenship. Cinthya had already been through this process, so she was able to help me get through everything with relative ease.

I am eternally thankful for all the things she did for me. It is because of her that I attended a great university. Because of her, I got to experience things that once seemed impossible. She gave me the tools necessary to succeed, and now I am able to help others the same way she helped me.

When Cinthya passed away, my mother and I visited Columbia University and met with several people who knew her. Her counselor spoke about her persistence when it came to school and about the friendship they formed. When Cinthya first met her counselor, she was working at a restaurant; appreciative of his help, she once took him a salad. He told her it was the best salad he had ever had and from that moment on, she took him food every time she visited him. She was the type of person who could form a friendship with anybody over anything, even food. We visited the pizza place where she worked to speak with her coworkers. I was approached by a man who told us that Cinthya was not just a coworker,

she was their friend. He mentioned that Cinthya would inform them about their rights, update them on current events regarding immigration, and even translate documents for them.

On behalf of my family, I would like to thank everyone who helped Cinthya throughout her life. Many of her strong aspirations and her success would not have been possible without the extended caring hands of those around her. Some went to extraordinary lengths to make sure my sister succeeded. It is people like that who give hope to millions of undocumented students in a time when our lives remain in a state of legal limbo. Even though Cinthya is no longer with us, the deep impression she made on all of us will continue to inspire every person she touched to reach new heights through education and advocacy.

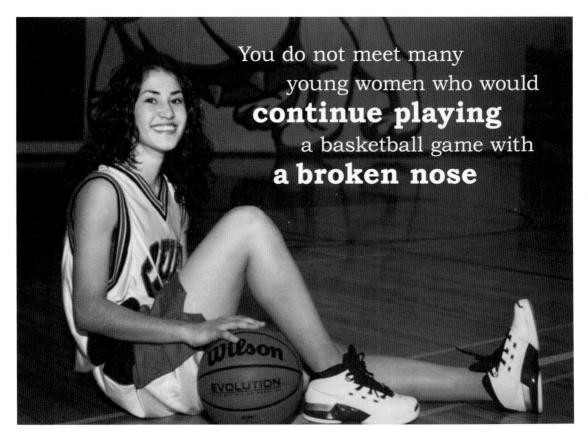

Cinthya at Garfield High School, 2003. *Courtesy of the Felix family.*

irreplaceable

Deana Duran

Edited by Rocio Trujillo

Cinthya was one of a kind, irreplaceable. You do not meet many young women who would wear their costumes the day after Halloween because they forgot to wear them the day of or who would continue playing a basketball game with a broken nose. But I was lucky enough to meet such a young woman. I had Cinthya.

Cinthya and I met our first year at Garfield High School. I was beginning my first year as an academic counselor at the school, while she was beginning her freshman year. I was her assistant basketball coach. Over our four years together at Garfield High, we developed a close friendship that I will never forget. I will always remember her as this young girl who would not stop talking or laughing. Even amid the struggle of coming to the United States and not knowing English, she remained determined and focused. Determined to learn English, her typical day consisted of school, basketball, and adult school from six o'clock to nine o'clock at night. She finished her ESL classes before the end of her second year in high school.

As our friendship grew stronger, I became Cinthya's mentor and role model, and she became mine. She visited me and demanded my help. I did my best to help her, but when the time came to apply for college, I did not know much about AB 540 or what I needed to do to help her. Cinthya and I researched AB 540 and learned the process together, step by step. Even after she left Garfield High, I did whatever I could to help her through the next steps of her life. I even helped her move into her dorm room as an undergraduate at UCLA.

More than anything, Cinthya taught me about life. Whenever I thought that my life was complicated, I would remember hers and realize mine was actually pretty easy. She always had a smile on her face, even when she was frustrated. Moreover, she always knew what she wanted and what to do to accomplish it. When Cinthya got accepted to Columbia University, she was ecstatic and even a little surprised, joking that maybe they had made a mistake. After waiting about a year before heading east, she left with no money, nowhere to stay, and no job, but with determination to start her master's program.

Cinthya wanted to do the master's program on her own. But the year she passed away, she was struggling, attending Columbia only part-time because she had to work two jobs to pay tuition. Despite the struggles, she kept working, and she kept going. She chose not to discuss her struggles with me. She talked more about working, living freely, and loving New York. She never asked for help while at Columbia, but I could see the struggle in her eyes. I supported her trips back and forth from New York, but I never asked her to pay me back. It was enough to witness her love and will to achieve the American dream.

Cinthya was an amazing person. She keeps me going when I am having a hard time. Just thinking about her motivates me to fight on. There is no doubt that Cinthya was one of a kind, irreplaceable.

a brave bruin:
opening doors for others at ucla

Jeff Cooper

In the summer of 2003, I was director of the UCLA Freshmen and Transfer Summer Programs (F/TSP), a six-week, rigorous academic program for entering freshmen and transfer students. Early in the program, Cinthya Felix, an incoming freshman, came to my office seeking help because she was unable to pay her fees and faced expulsion. She was so emotionally distressed that she was crying. She told me that her family was low-income and unable to pay the fees but that she had won a merit-based scholarship that would cover her fees, books, and living expenses. The problem was that UCLA would not release the $3,500 in scholarship money that she had competed for and won. This amount would have covered all of the program expenses. The Scholarship Office told her that the money, which had been sent to their office to be disbursed to Cinthya (following the normal process of scholarship distribution), was now "state money" by virtue of being in UCLA's hands. Since Cinthya was undocumented, the university was bound by law not to give her state money. I resolved the problem quickly by calling the donor who agreed to send a check for $3,500 to Cinthya's mother. I promised to have UCLA return the money to the donor, and the Scholarship Office complied with the request.

This was my first direct experience with an undocumented student at UCLA. I began to ask Cinthya many questions, and she began to educate me about the issues facing undocumented students in higher education in California. I knew that there had to be other undocumented students in the program who would probably also be coming from low-income families and that they would be facing similar obstacles. So after Cinthya left my office, I read as much as I could about the in-state tuition law, AB 540, and the politics surrounding its brief history. If I were going to help the undocumented students in my program, I would need to know the details of the law so that I could use it as a tool to support their efforts. Then I wrote a letter to the IRS in hope of eliminating some of the obstacles students face when trying to process scholarships.

Cinthya in Washington, DC, after a DREAM Act rally, spring 2007. *Courtesy of the Felix family.*

I also learned that most of the AB 540 undergraduate students at UCLA were in fact US citizens. More out-of-state citizens who had once lived in California benefit from this law than do undocumented students who currently live in the state. This was contrary to all of the views expressed in the media at that time—and even today—calling for repeal of this law.

After that initial meeting with Cinthya, a few more AB 540 undocumented students came to my office with the same problem: how to get the UCLA Scholarship Office to release the merit-based academic scholarships they had won. Later other students came because taxes were being deducted from their scholarship checks. This sounded illegal to me. I felt a sense of urgency. I realized that I needed to know just how many AB 540 undocumented students I had in the program. What about the students who would enter at the beginning of the academic year? They would need to know that there was a program—the Academic Advancement Program (AAP), the umbrella for F/TSP—that would be sensitive to their needs and aspirations and would support them in their quest for a degree at UCLA.

I contacted Cinthya because she had a strong and assertive character, was knowledgeable about AB 540, and had lots of experience overcoming all of the institutional barriers placed before her. She was articulate and had so much self-confidence that she would not be intimidated by top university administrators in face-to-face meetings. She could explain the key issues in a clear, concise, and cogent manner. Also Cinthya did not see herself in isolation from her community and her roots. She felt a strong connection with all students who were being treated unjustly, and she was willing and eager to fight for their needs.

Cinthya always responded to my requests for support, even for the tedious, lackluster, behind-the-scenes tasks. Every spring she helped my student staff call newly admitted students identified as possible AB 540 undocumented freshmen and transfer students. Cinthya spoke to these students and their parents and encouraged them to come to UCLA to pursue their bachelor's degrees. She spent countless evenings in March and April every year having lengthy conversations with them, answering all of their questions and encouraging them. She told them of the many opportunities at UCLA and invited them to become part of the growing undocumented student community. Cinthya helped run the AB 540 workshops at AAP's spring Scholars' Days for newly admitted students. After meeting students like Cinthya, other undocumented students were encouraged to enroll at UCLA. Cinthya responded to my requests to speak with AB 540 students who visited my office because they were facing crisis situations—academic, financial, family, psychological, or emotional. I always called on Cinthya to speak to students at all levels about the situations AB 540 undocumented students face and how they were successfully meeting the varied challenges before them. Cinthya always responded to these requests with great enthusiasm.

In the fall of 2003, when all the undocumented students we could identify first met, Cinthya played a leading role as spokesperson for the group. At the second meeting, drawing on the experiences of the group, Cinthya articulated the key issues that undocumented students faced on campus to top-level UCLA administrators. The message about UCLA staff mistreatment of undocumented students was hammered home and the administration promised to begin to address the issues and change staff attitudes. The problems with withholding the distribution of scholarships were addressed successfully. Students left those two meetings with greater confidence in themselves and in the university.

IDEAS was born in October 2003 out of these two meetings. Subsequently, student staff helped pull together resources for AB 540 undocumented students. Cinthya and a few other students played a key role in creating the resource guidebook that went out under the name of IDEAS. Cinthya played a seminal role in many other impressive projects that were produced by IDEAS, and she was always present and willing to work hard on behalf of her fellow students. Cinthya inspired others with her positive attitude in the face of adversity and encouraged students to set their goals at the highest mark.

The Cinthya Felix who came to my office crying in 2003 was not a person to ever give up—on herself or on others. She was a brave person. She was the first person to push open the door for others and help light their way. After our initial meeting, I never again saw her in such a low emotional state. Our later contacts were always political, always about confronting the pressing issues facing AB 540 undocumented students.

I never got to know Cinthya socially—to see her lighter, more relaxed, joyful, and wilder side. However, ours was a rich, meaningful relationship. We were able to solve important social and economic problems for her fellow students because we respected each other's commitment to social justice. I am not exaggerating when I say that Cinthya enriched my life. She strengthened my resolve to meet all the challenges thrown up by the system. Her tireless efforts encouraged me to work harder, and they gave me more hope that all of us can change restrictive and discriminatory laws. In all struggles, we need role models; we need to know that we are not alone, that we have others who will support our work. Cinthya was a comrade in this struggle. I will always miss her.

She was the **first person** to push
open the door for others
and help
light their way

big dreams in the big apple

Nancy Mejia

The story of Cinthya Felix in New York City is one of determination. During her time there, I think many were unaware of the magnitude of her struggle. In fact for many, her memorial services were the first exposure they had to this side of Cinthya. In contemplating why this may have been, I remember a conversation she and I once had. We were sitting on our big brown couch in our pajamas, having one of those late-night conversations that always happened when she had an assignment due the next day: our procrastination bonding sessions. We were reminiscing about our days as undergraduates at UCLA—which usually turned into a Columbia University-bashing session—and in this particular instance, Cinthya was expressing her frustration with her lack of a support system. She said that it went beyond curricular support and went on to explain that while at UCLA, she was a member of the group IDEAS, which formally fought for the rights of undocumented students and informally served as a strong support network for these students inside and outside of the classroom. Cinthya's experience as an undocumented student at Columbia up until that point had been daunting, administratively and financially. Although she had faced that before, she was not used to facing it alone. Cinthya was part of a one-woman minority at the School of

Cinthya on the Brooklyn Bridge. *Courtesy of the Felix family.*

Public Health, so many of her battles were fought behind closed doors, not on a campus quad or in a march.

Because this is the story I think she would have liked to share with other undocumented students, I would like to tell you the colorful and vivid story of the Cinthya who went to New York City simply to be a student. Although New York may not have been ready for Cinthya the activist, it did not stop her from leaving a big fat mark.

Cinthya saw a master's in public health as a gateway into a career in health. She was particularly interested in working to reduce the health disparities that Latino immigrant populations faced. She chose to study sociomedical sciences, the discipline in public health that explores the

with none of the options that her prospective classmates could take advantage of. She was at a crossroads because while she had a professional and personal interest in attending a renowned Ivy League graduate program, she could not afford it. For anyone else, this may have seemed like an impossible situation, but not for Cinthya. If there is anything you should take away from her life story, this is it: Cinthya had a way of turning the greatest obstacle into an opportunity. Rather than withdrawing her application, she notified Columbia University that she would be deferring admission for a year, so she could work and fund-raise diligently to finance her first year in New York City. She was ready to enroll in the fall of 2008.

> If there is anything you should take away from her life story, this is it: Cinthya had a **way** of turning the **greatest obstacle** into an **opportunity**

impact of social contexts on health behaviors and outcomes. But upon receiving her acceptance to Columbia's MPH (Master of Public Health) program for the fall 2007 semester, Cinthya's excitement turned to worry. Enrolling in the program meant paying about $20,000 in tuition and $15,000 in living expenses per year for two years, not to mention books and other personal expenses, like travel to California and clothing. Although the high cost of graduate school is a common dilemma for many, it is usually resolved by turning to federal and private aid, most commonly in the form of student loans. For Cinthya, however, this was not an option. Because of her immigration status, she was not eligible for any type of credit—no federal student loans, no private loans, and no credit cards—leaving her

I met Cinthya in September of 2008. My supervisor had received an e-mail from an old friend and Cinthya's UCLA professor and mentor, Kent Wong. He asked my supervisor to look out for Cinthya in her transition to the East Coast and extend any support that she could, particularly with work or scholarship opportunities, because aside from being new to the city, she was undocumented. At the bottom of his e-mail, he included a link to her fund-raising page. I remember thinking, "fund-raising page?" and clicked on the link. I was both moved and impressed by what I saw. In a carefully crafted message, Cinthya laid out her story—of her past and ongoing struggles as an undocumented student, her determination to pursue a professional career in medicine, and her immediate goal to study public health—and prompted readers to help her reach her goal by providing a donation. I sent her an e-mail introducing myself and offering to help with anything she needed. I also made a donation. That was classic Cinthya, resourceful and convincing. She had your ear the minute she opened her mouth, and she took advantage of every minute of your attention, whether to get a point across, to defend her cause, or to involve you in her amusement. It was impossible to turn away from her and say no, because she simply would not let you.

Since I had made the move from west to east a few years before and had recently finished the MPH program at Columbia University, it only felt natural to reach out to her. In my e-mail to her, I mentioned that I had a room available for rent in my apartment. Minutes later, I had an enthusiastic full-page response in which she confessed how relieved she was to find someone from Los Angeles—especially someone who knew the meaning of AB 540; she had been through a rough first week in New York City. She was excited to hear about the room and asked to see it that evening. Five hours later, she was standing at my front door. Although it only took her two minutes to decide she wanted to rent the room, we spent the next four hours talking. We talked about her adventures staying at hostels and couch surfing and the disappointments of apartment hunting in New York; about her introduction to the good, the bad, and the ugly of Columbia University; about her childhood in Mexico and her young adulthood in the United States; about her cherished UCLA years; about her past and ongoing struggles as an undocumented student; and about her immediate goals and big dreams. She moved in the next day, and that is how Cinthya found her home in New York.

When she first approached the financial aid office about her need to cover the cost of tuition for the two-year MPH program, the financial aid officers were dumbfounded and even questioned the legality of her enrolling as a student. That is to say that Cinthya learned very early on that she was an anomaly at the school and would have to do a lot of advocating for herself—with administration, faculty, and fellow classmates.

Her frustration with the school grew and time and time again, I listened to her vent about their inability to help her financially; each time she went to speak with financial aid officers, she was given a different excuse ending in "no." At one point they proposed she obtain a student visa, but the visa would expire come graduation, at which point she would have to leave the country. Cinthya could not accept that a public school like UCLA was able to assist her, but a wealthy, private university could not, so she pressed on. She eventually learned that she was the only undocumented student to have ever enrolled in the program, and that is why the administration did not know how to help her financially. Cinthya was stunned and enraged, but she used the circumstance as an opportunity to open some tightly closed doors at Columbia. For weeks she struggled with the financial aid office and other school administrators, educating them about the different ways they could legally award aid to students like her. She called on administrators and faculty she had known at UCLA to advocate on her behalf. Many confrontations later, Columbia offered her a small scholarship toward the cost of her tuition.

When a friend told Cinthya of a job that would be opening up at a pizza restaurant, she jumped at the opportunity. She worked at that restaurant for over a year as a hostess, taking phone orders, and as a waitress. But her income from the restaurant work wasn't enough; she was barely managing to pay rent and her monthly bills, and she was also trying to provide financial support to her family back home in Los Angeles. She had the cost of another year of tuition hanging over her head, so when an additional job opportunity presented itself, she went for it. One of my former classmates who worked at the National Center for Disaster Preparedness (NCDP) was over for dinner one night, and he told Cinthya and me about a new project that he was helping to launch at his job. Cinthya provided him with several contacts and went on to advise him on a number of things that the center should consider in carrying out the project, both in designing the investigation and in collecting the data. He offered her a part-time research assistant position.

Between these two jobs and other occasional work, like speaking on panels or per diem research assistance, Cinthya was working the equivalent of a full-time workweek in addition to being a full-time student. As extraordinary and determined as she was in balancing her responsibilities, this schedule became too demanding and took a toll on her energy, focus, and achievement. On an average weekday, she went to NCDP in the morning and then rushed off to the restaurant in the afternoon. She made it back to the apartment usually after midnight and woke up early the next day to go to class. It was a tough routine to maintain, and although she could endure it, Cinthya ultimately found herself in a difficult place. On the one hand, she had to work in order to pay for school and rent; on the other hand, she was spending so much time trying to make ends meet that she was left with little time to study and prepare for her classes. She performed this balancing act until she reached the end of her first year in the MPH program. She had fallen too far behind in some of her classes, and for the first time in her life, she finished the school year with two incompletes. Cinthya was filled with disappointment and began to question whether staying in the program was worth the sacrifice.

Although Cinthya had told me about some of her disappointments with her graduate school experience, I did not realize how much it had affected her until then. Having gone through the MPH program myself, I could understand her frustrations with the homogeneous student body, the limited consciousness on issues that mattered to us and the communities we represented, and the inability to relate with other students and faculty. But there was one thing that constantly haunted her and made her feel out of place—her sense of insecurity about the future. For Cinthya, her life goals were all dependent on one piece of legislation. Without the DREAM Act's passage, she could not see the future she had worked so hard for, so her time at Columbia became her limbo. If she didn't continue the program, she saw that first year as wasted time and money, and she was unsure of her next move. If she continued, she feared that she would be wasting time and money on the remainder of the program, because she was not sure how it would help her make her next move. Either way, she did not have the privilege that most of her peers did, of going through school knowing that a career was on the horizon.

Cinthya was also disappointed at how little support the university had offered her and how draining the process had been. She could not understand how this could happen at an institution situated in one of the most diverse urban centers of the world. "How can New York be so behind on the immigrant student rights' agenda?!" she used to ask in astonishment. What seemed to frustrate her the most is that she found herself alone in that fight. Although she had a diverse group of friends who were supportive and sympathetic to her circumstance, they could not relate to her on the level that mattered most to Cinthya: being undocumented. As if that weren't disheartening enough, none of the student groups at the school was tackling the issue. She often told me how difficult her experience at Columbia was primarily because she lacked the support system she had come to know through professors and other dreamers at UCLA.

Cinthya found solace in her old friends who had been a part of her UCLA network. During one of Tam's visits, Cinthya became acquainted with a network of undergraduate students who were organizing events in support of the DREAM Act. I remember Cinthya telling me about the group and how thrilled she was to participate in the planning of the events, trying to raise awareness at Columbia University in the months leading up to the congressional vote on the DREAM Act. Cinthya attended their meetings for a few weeks, and she seemed enthusiastic about the events they had planned, but I also remember her disappointment. She was frustrated by the fear that was impeding the group; many of the students were undocumented and were scared to go public with their stories, not knowing what reaction to expect from school officials or their peers. Cinthya had been through this when she and her UCLA classmates were starting IDEAS, and so she tried to advise and motivate the group with stories of her experience. But in the end, they were not ready to take that stance.

In the fall of 2009, Cinthya enrolled in her third semester. Around that time, she reached out to the Office of Student Affairs, and this became her safe haven at Columbia. I remember the sense of relief she felt after talking to them about her daily struggles during the previous year, and her discussions with them helped her to also open up with faculty. For a while, Cinthya avoided talking to her professors about the difficulties she was having, out of fear that they would think she was an inept or lazy student. When she finally met with them, she told me that she felt a huge weight lifted off her shoulders, because their reactions had been very understanding and supportive. She felt a new sense of encouragement to stay in the program and excel, and so she worked with the Student Affairs Office on an academic plan for the remainder of her MPH studies. The plan was that she would finish the program as a part-time student in the spring of 2011, and upon clearing her incompletes, the school would cover the cost of her remaining tuition. I remember how elated she was to hear this, especially given the administrative greeting she had received when she first arrived at Columbia. Regrettably, I'm not sure how many people she was able to celebrate this triumph with though, given the sensitivity of the matter for her and for the university.

Having been witness to Cinthya's life in New York as her roommate, friend, and pseudo big sister, I couldn't pass up the opportunity for a final act of praise for the legacy that she left behind. A similar feeling must have driven the speeches at the memorial held for her at Columbia. Faculty and Student Affairs administrators described her as a very ambitious, curious, and dedicated student, and they spoke of their admiration for her resilient spirit and determination to succeed. They spoke about how proud they felt that she was a student in the program and confessed they were all rooting for her to succeed. They looked forward to seeing her walk across the commencement stage, because they knew she had worked so hard for it.

On May 21, 2010, the dean of students awarded Cinthya Nathalie Felix a posthumous master's degree in public health.

Cinthya in New York. *Courtesy of the Felix family.*

THE SEATTLE UNDERGROUND RAILROAD

> "The state wants our money, so they let us buy the car, get insurance, and pay for registration. But when it comes to giving us a license, they dont want to give you one."

UCLA Sophomore

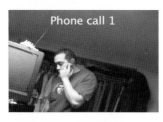
Phone call 1

All the DMV's in Seattle are booked.

So we drive three hours to Ellensburg to take the driving test.

Is the address you want your license mailed to in Seattle?

> "**Yes**, I got my ID!"
>
> "I think this is my **proudest** moment as a Washingtonian."

UCLA Junior

ID'S: 3 down
LICENSES: 3 to go

"We had **three goals** to accomplish before we left Seattle: to get our IDs, to pass our written tests for our licenses and **most important**, to get our driver's licenses."

Cynthia taking driving test

matias's test

"Having a license has been so helpful for me. Now I can **prove** that I'm Cinthya and I'm 22 years old."

Stills from *The Seattle Underground Railroad*,
Tram Tran, 2007.

my daughter's journey

Loc Thi Pham

Translated by Thai Le; *edited by* Helen Yi

I always told Tam that being undocumented meant that we had to work harder than other people. It meant we were different. She understood this and took it as a challenge. She was not discouraged and instead worked hard and excelled in everything she did. While my daughter Tam was obedient and respectful, once she decided to do something, she would do it.

Our stay in Germany was a difficult time for our family because we could not afford a babysitter nor teach Tam in a language that was also new to us. And even though our neighborhood had a relatively

Tam with her mother in Germany, 1982.
Courtesy of the Tran family.

large Vietnamese population, we did not have any family or close friends. There were times when my husband and I had to leave Tam and her younger brother Lolly alone while we worked. Tam was so brave and took care of Lolly by the time she was five. My daughter was always so smart. I remember when I taught her how to ride a bicycle. We started out with training wheels, but she did not need them for long.

I still do not understand why we were considered undocumented once we arrived in the United States. We were essentially stateless when we applied for asylum. I know a lot of other people who emigrated from Vietnam, but they have documents. I never exposed myself by telling people I did not have paperwork; I hid. But Tam was not like that. She said we needed to tell people so that they could help us. Tam soon became familiar with the system and helped us get temporary work permits each year.

Tam graduated from Santa Ana Community College and was accepted into UCLA. I was overjoyed, but I was also scared. She had to move away from us in Orange County and rent an apartment near the campus. She was also apprehensive about living there, but mainly because of the cost. Tam always tried to lighten our family's financial burdens. I did help her with the rent the first couple of months she was there but with her tenacity, she quickly found a job that would help her pay for tuition and rent. Because I did not have access to transportation, I was not able to visit Tam in Los Angeles as often as I would have liked.

With her mother at Tam's UCLA graduation, 2007. *Courtesy of the Tran family.*

Her drive to continue her education was unstoppable. She told me she wanted to be a lawyer at one point. Later I found out that she said this to make me happy. Her actual goal was to become a professor, and she was on her way to achieving this at Brown University. She also said that she wanted to help people like us who were in our same situation.

I regret the time I had to spend working long shifts, some that lasted from Monday morning to Saturday night. It was time that I did not get to see my daughter grow up, and now that time has run out. As I look through her pictures, I can see how happy she was to be herself—never bored and always on the verge of a new adventure. She was so beautiful and simply enjoyed life. I am very proud of all that my daughter accomplished.

She was so beautiful and **simply enjoyed life**. I am very proud of all that my **daughter accomplished.**

my only sister

Thien "Lolly" Tran
Edited by Helen Yi

Growing up with Tam as my older sister made life easier. She shouldered all the responsibilities, all the time. She tried her best not to let our undocumented status affect me the way that I felt it had affected her. I knew we were undocumented, but that was the extent of it. I did not even find out that our asylum case got rejected until years after the decision was made. That's how it was for me; I was shielded from these issues.

Because our lives were defined by our immigration status, Tam worked hard and wanted me to work hard as well. She believed in getting an education, and she constantly encouraged me to go to school. Unaware of AB 540, I thought that I could never afford the cost of Santa Ana College. When I told Tam that it was simply too much money, she dragged me back to the community college and informed the cashier's office that I qualified for in-state tuition because of AB 540.

When Tam left for UCLA, I just could not believe it. The fact that she got accepted was not the surprising part. What awed me the most was that, given our situation, she still found a way to pursue education at the university level. It was a huge accomplishment in my eyes. Tam's passion for her work also inspired me. I had never seen her as proud as she was at the premiere of her film, *Lost and Found*. Seeing her that day made me want to experience those same feelings and that sense of accomplishment.

Our status made it difficult to acquire work permits. We had to renew our permits every year, but because our case was quite unique, our renewal always depended on who handled it. It was hard for immigration officials to understand that while our family was Vietnamese, we were German immigrants, and neither country would take us back. Sometimes we had to wait weeks before the matter got resolved. After years of struggling with this issue, we fixed it, but not before my entire family was detained. This happened after Tam testified in front of Congress about her immigration status. While we were proud of her, we did not think that people were going to take her seriously. Then ICE agents staged a raid and detained my parents and me for three days.

Tam with her younger brother Lolly at the Santa Ana zoo, 1992.
Courtesy of the Tran family.

We grew concerned about Tam's candidness about our situation, but at the same time, it was her openness and connections that helped us get out of detention and get our work permits, without having to fear that we may again get rejected. However, we also have a pending deportation order. It could happen any day of the week or anytime during the year. Something like this really affects your state of mind—that dark cloud hanging above your head, never knowing when it is going to start pouring down on you.

Before Tam passed away, I was not involved in the immigrant youth movement. She took me to a few events and demonstrations, but I did not see the purpose. My parents and I always wondered why Tam was devoting so much of her time to it. At one point, I was even ready to give up school altogether, but now Tam is my motivation to continue with my education and stay involved with the cause. After she passed, I became more active by attending more meetings and events. The movement has really gained momentum because of all the students, allies, and other supporters. I met many of them when I participated in the 2010 Tour de Dreams promoting immigrant rights—a 540-mile bike ride from Berkeley to Los Angeles—on the same bike that my sister used for the previous year's trek.

I would like to thank the people who were friends with my sister and those who are carrying on the fight that she could not finish. Life without Tam is difficult, but she still provides a lot of the inspiration for our family and many others. She is my driving force. I am also grateful for all the letters from people I have never met. The surge of support that our family received has been amazing. It will not be forgotten.

I would like to **thank** the people who were friends with my sister and those who are **carrying on the fight** that she could not finish

The Tran family is recognized by the Coalition for Humane Immigrant Rights of Los Angeles after Tam's testimony before Congress, 2007. *Courtesy of the Tran family.*

We cannot control when life ends
But we are here today, family and friends
To celebrate the girl behind the lens
To celebrate the best German import since Mercedes-Benz
We're celebrating Tam Tran, I'm sure you've seen her
Is it physically possible to not love this active DREAMer?
The one with her hair pushed back behind her ear
The one filled with such bright IDEAS
She did it without financial aid, without an edge
Yet she still graduated from Santa Ana College
Since higher education was what she was pursuing
It all made sense when she became a UCLA Bruin
And that's how she earned her cap and gown
But then she had to go "Underground at Brown"
Cause she was told by immigration agents that her time here was rented
But that's how it is when you're undocumented
So she went nationwide for the world to see
And caused all kinds of trouble in Washington, DC
With all her soul she fought so hard
And all she ever wanted was a green card
Her life mission is complete, she should take a bow
Because she doesn't need one where she is right now
She battled so intensely, like a true samurai
The difference is she's only "Armed with a Camera"
Pass the DREAM act! How sweet the sound
Because right now it's in the "Lost and Found"
What a tremendous life, I know we'll all miss her
I will dedicate my life to my only sister

—Thien "Lolly" Tran

Lolly Tran mourns and celebrates his sister's life, May 2011. *Courtesy of Pocho1.*

what tam tran taught a professor of american history

Tom Osborne

Until my retirement in 2009, I taught American history at Santa Ana College and several other universities for forty years. Every once in a while, I had a student who unintentionally taught me, challenging me to rethink course content and my original impression of the student, who outwardly seemed no different from others in my classrooms. Such a student was Ms. Tam Tran.

I first met Tam, a bright-eyed, quietly energetic, young Vietnamese woman, when she enrolled in my US History since the Civil War honors seminar at Santa Ana College in 2002. She was the top student in the class, and her essays were models of clarity, logic, and insight. With a background in the history of American foreign relations, I saw to it that students were exposed to America's deeds and misdeeds overseas, strongly focusing on US empire-building in the Pacific basin, beginning with the Spanish-American War. As an opponent of the Vietnam War, I taught my students about Lyndon Johnson's groundless claim regarding a second Gulf of Tonkin attack, the Pentagon Papers revelations, and the My Lai Massacre. Tam came to my office shortly after our seminar discussion of these matters and said that from the standpoint of Vietnamese boat people, America's war in Southeast Asia had at least one positive consequence: it provided a means for victims of Vietnamese communists to get out of the country and immigrate to the United States.

She caught me off guard. I had never thought of how the war might look to such victims, who certainly have a legitimate point of view. To this day, I see the Vietnam War (or the American War, as people in Vietnam call it) as a colossal mistake for the United States, for many reasons. But Tam forced me to think about that conflict from another perspective, that of families like her own who were and remain grateful for the opportunity that the war afforded them to live better lives in the United States. If by circumstances of history and geography, I had been a Vietnamese refugee, I could see how my view of the war might have been dictated by that plight. This is a profound lesson that the student taught the professor. I learned that the truths of history are many-sided and at times conflicting and even paradoxical.

Outside of the classroom especially, I learned much from Tam. As the principal faculty advisor to Santa Ana College's chapter of Phi Theta Kappa, the national community college honor society, I had the task in 2003 of replacing our chapter's president. Tam, our vice president, was extremely reluctant to take over the duties of acting president. I saw that she was shy, quiet, intensely focused on earning high grades, and scrambling to find enough part-time work to buy books. I did not see her as an ideal candidate to take over the running of our nationally recognized chapter of Phi Theta Kappa, yet no one else stepped forward.

Desperate, I practically begged Tam to take the presidency, promising to help and assuring her that she had the makings of a fine chapter president. This went on for a week or so; I'm not even sure that I believed what I was telling her, so eager was I to fill the vacancy and keep our chapter moving ahead. At the time, I had not the slightest inkling that sitting before me in my office was a young woman of extraordinary promise as a national leader who would one day be testifying before Congress. That she reluctantly agreed to be chapter president was enough for me at the time. The two of us would somehow make this work.

Within a few weeks of taking on the presidency, Tam's leadership and people skills advanced by leaps and bounds. No longer did I need to advise her; my co-advisor, the other officers, and chapter members saw clearly that Tam was in charge and superbly organized. She initiated a series of garage sales to raise scholarship funds and effectively delegated tasks among the officers. At the end of her presidency in spring 2004, our chapter had raised $1,000 for scholarships thanks to Tam's creativity and leadership. I was astonished at how she juggled a full academic load (carrying a 3.8 grade point average), part-time employment,

and student leadership—never complaining about the heavy schedule.

Through her presidency of our Phi Theta Kappa chapter, Tam taught me that some of our students were extraordinary people who had achieved academically under circumstances more dire than I ever imagined. The longer I taught at Santa Ana College, the more I came to see that I hardly knew our students. I regularly read the statistical handouts on family income and educational levels that came my way courtesy of our college's research office. Getting to know Tam, however, opened my eyes to our Vietnamese students from immigrant families settling in Orange County after 1975. These families were pursuing the American dream of educational opportunity and a better life; their sons and daughters assimilated fast and excelled in their classes.

Even so, those who through no fault of their own were undocumented found that outstanding grades did not grant them access to publicly funded scholarships. Moreover, postgraduate job prospects

With her mother at Tam's Santa Ana College graduation, 2003. *Courtesy of the Tran family.*

I had not the slightest inkling that sitting before me was a young woman of **extraordinary promise** as a national leader who would one day be **testifying before Congress**

remained uncertain for these high achievers. My undocumented students who entered and won statewide and national competitions for scholarships at times succumbed to pressure from their own families to reject substantial cash awards because the resulting newspaper publicity could lead to deportation. These students, the best at our community college, would have stood out at Berkeley or UCLA or Pomona, at the most demanding institutions. Even when they transferred to such places, our undocumented students had to navigate the confusing, roiled waters of immigration regulations, translate for and protect their parents, and keep body and mind together, while working part-time or more and earning the highest marks, just in case a graduate degree might be obtainable. This was Tam's rugged path.

This too has been the path of successive generations of immigrants coming to America. Like many of them, she saved practically every paycheck for her education. She embodied the American dream of hard work, thrift, and giving back. In terms of intelligence, character, a deep understanding of American culture, and the filmmaking brilliance to portray the lives of undocumented students, Tam far outshone the putative "best and brightest" who enter prestigious colleges with their silver spoons still firmly planted in their mouths. Tam understood that the promise of America has always been the opportunities it afforded "the tempest-tossed" from other lands to rise on the basis of their merits and work ethic. Her career goal was to teach at a community college to help others faced with her challenges. What could be more American than Tam's story? After a lifetime of studying and writing about US history, it took Tam to help me struggle with my cynicism about the materialism and vanities of our society. Through her indefatigable campaigning to organize our nation's undocumented youth, Tam opened my eyes to see that the American promise is truly alive and nowhere more so than in the DREAM Act.

How privileged I was to have my student Tam Tran take my education as a historian of American culture to a deeper level. I will be forever in her debt, and she will be forever in my heart.

the girl behind the camera

Stephanie Solis

When my friend Tam casually raised the question about whether I would be comfortable as the subject of her upcoming film about the experience of being undocumented, the word "documentary" never came up. She cheerfully asked, "Hey, could I follow you around for a while and just film you being Stephanie? I'll buy you lunch!" Okay, I thought, this seemed loose enough. Tam and I had met in 2006 through IDEAS at UCLA. After finding humor in our situations and joking about the parallels between IDEAS students and the X-Men, we became fast friends.

I was used to seeing her carry around a little handheld digital camera like an extension of her arm. But when she showed up at my apartment that first morning at seven o'clock with her camera, tripod, lighting setup, laptop, bags full of digital videotapes, a black background tarp the size of a swimming pool cover, boundless early-morning energy, and zero coffee, I began to realize there was something else to her personality. Tam's fun, casual attitude was able to coexist with an over-arching professionalism in a way that, to me in my pajama pants, seemed paradoxical. Wisecracking twenty-somethings with hip haircuts and indie-rock reference points don't typically get up at the crack of dawn of their own accord—especially not to collect interview footage of some girl from campus, a nobody, and certainly not about a dry, relatively uncelebrated immigration rights issue. But it turned out I was approaching the subject in entirely the wrong way.

The final edit of the documentary *Lost and Found* opens with me talking about my childhood photos. This was a decision I struggled with and fought Tam on during the editing process. Prior to that first morning of filming, she suggested that I find some of my baby photos to use in the video. I had only a few to choose from because my family and I lost most of our possessions and photos that were in a public storage unit when I was a teenager. She asked me to explain this incident as she filmed me. I didn't expect it to end up in the final video; after all, it was a weird, semidepressing, random factoid of my youth that had nothing to do with the DREAM Act. She ended up not only including the incident but also making it the centerpiece of the film. I told her about my reservations. I said it felt distracting and had no real ties to the issue of immigration. I thought its inclusion made the video seem like two completely unrelated "Unfortunate Things in One Person's Life." Tam brightly said, "No, it's perfect, it fits really well," while eating an enormous mouthful of frozen yogurt, and she did not explain her motives much further.

Eventually I came around and realized what she was doing with the video. She had created a perfect narrative parallel between being undocumented and not possessing anything. It wasn't just an interesting story-telling trick. The parallel invited viewers to imagine something that could conceivably happen to themselves or to anyone they knew—a loss of possessions in a burglary or fire—and mentally tie it to the experience of being undocumented.

Maybe I was too close to the subject matter. Maybe I didn't trust Tam's judgment enough at that point. Or maybe I hadn't read enough basic film criticism. Regardless of the reason, it wasn't until I had seen *Lost and Found* approximately thirty billion times that I realized why she edited it the

Every voicemail message Tam left me over the last five years ended the same way: "It'll be fuuuuuun. Call me!" There was always that same encouraging intonation. For five years, we had gone to various events together to tell our respective immigration experiences in support of the DREAM Act.

I was used to seeing her carry around a little handheld **digital camera** like an **extension of her arm**

way she did. Then I started to develop a better understanding of how her mind worked, her insight, and the enormous impact she had on so many people. Luckily for me, it was easy to see the video thirty billion times, thanks to what Tam jokingly called The Tam and Stephanie Show.

The settings varied wildly. Sometimes the "show" would literally be a show, speaking at a press conference or being interviewed by a nationally syndicated television news program. Other times we would be at a small church banquet hall in a town I had never heard of.

Tam and Stephanie working on *Lost and Found. Courtesy of Stephanie Solis*

Sometimes we spoke to classes, often right at UCLA. Once we received an honorarium to share, a small amount of money in exchange for speaking to the class. "Honorarium," she said in that encouraging tone. I had no idea what that word meant and had to Google it. It sounded like a musical instrument. But Tam somehow figured out her way around academia and its insides, and she used words like "honorarium" and "stipend" and "work-study" and "research" with a capital "R," words that awed me. Her ability to navigate and work the system, rather than become overwhelmed or overlooked by it, totally baffled me. But it made me trust her, always.

The Tam and Stephanie Show was composed of an introduction, screening the documentary, our personal testimonials, and information on the DREAM Act. My story was more or less identical every time. I brought notes, developed a performer's glazed expression, and used the same five jokes to overcompensate for what I worried would come off as five to ten minutes of scripted self-pity to the wrong listener. Tam would be next. She was completely different—no script, no jokes. Her straightforward, unpretentious honesty was somehow both completely easygoing and totally devastating. "Hey everybody, so here's my deal," she seemed to be saying, conversationally running through her immigration story totally impromptu, like it was not a story at all, but just her life.

In short, that was the magic of how Tam communicated with people. She was so unedited and without pretense that she was completely disarming. Even the rhythm of her voice—she used the same easygoing voice in testimonials that she used with her friends—cut through the stuffy formality of a press conference or the United States Congress like a knife. Her candidness was so head-on, so profoundly effective at bringing outsiders in to understand and support the DREAM Act. And I realized what she was getting across to people: We are insiders, and we are part of America. This was the idea she drove home effortlessly, without once seeming like she was trying to drive it home.

An insider and an outsider, a cool nerd, a filmmaker whose own life should have been on the other side of the camera, Tam embodied so many seemingly incongruous traits as though it were nothing unusual at all. Everyone who met her had to reevaluate a hundred crushed stereotypes at once. Then the stereotypes became meaningless. She was a one-woman eye-opener, a heart-opener, and a mind-opener; those who met her had "the Tam Tran experience." And that feeling completely captivated everyone she met.

Sometimes I feel like I have never fully grasped the impact Tam had on so many people. I noticed that even after she left for Brown University and was less often physically present at Los Angeles DREAM Act events, the name Tam Tran was in the air. I would literally overhear it in the roar of conversations, as I made my way through crowds. It was funny to me how much could be inferred from the use of her full name: it meant that the speaker was not a personal friend of hers, who would have just called her Tam, but they knew who she was nevertheless. Tam Tran. Tam Tran. I wonder from time to time when her name actually represents her as a person and when it represents an idea, the DREAM Act itself. Once in a while that worries me, but I feel like she would just say, "No, it's perfect, it fits really well," with a mouthful of frozen yogurt. So I will trust her, always. Tam Tran. Tam Tran. Sometimes it sounds like one word to me at this point. I still overhear it in the roar of the crowds, and as time goes on, I hear the roar deepen.

lost and found

"I am 18 years old, and I don't exist.... Being undocumented feels like you're a kid forever."

"I'm in America because disco died.... My dad's job was installing and maintaining the sound systems for all the discos in Manila."

"Since I'm not eligible for financial aid, it's really hit or miss when I can or can't be in school"

"You're holding children hostage, and nobody ever remembers the children."

"Nobody looks at that little girl and thinks, What happens to that girl when she grows up?"

Every year 65,000 to 80,000 undocumented students graduate from high school.

Stills from *Lost and Found*, Tran Tran, 2007.

an ivy league of her own

Matthew Garcia

And God stepped out on space,
And He looked around and said,
"I'm lonely—
I'll make me a world."
　　—James Weldon Johnson,
　　"The Creation"

African American artists have often drawn on James Weldon Johnson's poem as an explanation of the world they had to create for themselves in order to make their unique contributions to the culture we share in this country. I have always thought this quote applied to Tam and how she created a world for her friends and herself to thrive in. This was the case before she arrived at Brown University, and it was certainly true of her life in Providence, Rhode Island.

Tam arrived at Brown as an accomplished filmmaker who had produced two impressive films, *Lost and Found* and *The Seattle Underground Railroad*. By incorporating the right mix of music and images in a *cinema vérité* style, Tam captured the dilemma of undocumented youth in this country and their unique place in the world today. As many in the immigrant student rights movement know better than I, the films have become a primary vehicle for advocacy and education pertaining to the DREAM Act. *Lost and Found* in particular has circulated widely on the Internet. The film's brief but powerful documentation of the life of her friend and fellow undocumented student, Stephanie Solis, offers a window into the dilemma that these students face. Tam rarely appeared

on film, preferring to be "the girl behind the camera," where she was always more comfortable. Her approach to filmmaking mirrored her humble, self-effacing style of activism. She helped reveal a world formerly invisible to peers who had the privilege of being documented.

These films were my introduction to Tam Tran. She included them as part of her application to our graduate program in the Department of American Civilization at Brown University. I had the good fortune of sitting on the admissions committee the year that we chose to admit her. I found the films so moving that I immediately showed them to my classes, not knowing whether she would accept our invitation to join us at Brown. The films inspired many students, including some who had already begun to think about issues related to undocumented students. Tam's depiction of the lives of students from a variety of backgrounds also offered a vision of interethnic coalition politics that many were hungry for on our campus.

Tam accepted our invitation and attended our recruitment day. Her trip included a visit to Yale University, where she had also been accepted. I recognized Tam as a perfect student for our program, given her freewheeling, interdisciplinary, multimedia approach to studying American culture. Yet, given the enormous prestige and wealth of Yale, it is often difficult for young people to make a decision solely based on how well the program fits their interests. Tam, however, got it. I talked to her about the large and diverse immigrant population in Providence that would make her feel at home, about the many professors who cared deeply about her subject and would treat her as though she were family, and about the cohort of students who would offer her a support system during her life away from California. We also hit it off on a personal level given my Southern California roots and her desire to learn more about the world she came from. In typical Tam fashion, she told me she would let her "vibe" direct her, and fortunately it pointed her to Brown University.

Tam had an ability to speak across generational, class, and racial lines. She

Tam with the Brown Immigrant Rights Coalition, October 2009. *Courtesy of the Brown Immigrant Rights Coalition.*

frequently organized events highlighting the shared struggles of immigrants in venues ranging from academia and student group meetings to community organizations and local schools. During an event at Brown University, she brought a group of activists, including Cinthya, to talk about the experience that undocumented immigrants face in education. The event was an academic conference attended by mostly number-crunching social scientists; however, when she and a group of Asian and Latino students spoke, she moved everyone to tears and brought all the participants to their feet by the end. She often talked to me about her profound connection to Latino youth, and she conducted programs in local schools for parents and students worried about accessing a college education. Tam also played

an important role in creating the student group, Brown Immigrant Rights Coalition (BIRC). Working with mostly undergraduate and local high-school students, Tam and BIRC convinced Rhode Island politicians to support the rights of undocumented students. BIRC continues today as the primary advocacy group in Rhode Island for the passage of the DREAM Act.

As a graduate student, Tam was often quiet in class, but her mind was always working. When we met one-on-one, we had conversations that I don't believe I have ever had with any student. She often talked about her love for filmmaking, and we discussed at great length how that talent might later blossom into a transformative force within the profession through her own productions. In her scholarship, she was beginning to document the trajectory and power of student politics over the last half century. She merged historical inquiry with participant observation, an approach indicative of a true interdisciplinary scholar. Given the vision and experience she had as an activist and filmmaker, she knew exactly what her contribution would be to academia. Her intention to explain the place of the current student immigrant rights movement within the history of student movements dating back to the founding of the Students for a Democratic Society (SDS) would have transformed the way we think about several fields of study, including youth studies, social movements, and immigrant rights. Her knowledge and experience, combined with her commitment to explore ideas in various media, including writing, film, and exhibition, helped her advisors and peers to recognize how scholars must be versatile in communicating big, challenging ideas to a digital and image-oriented world.

Tam was a great friend who possessed a moral force that compelled us all to be more generous human beings with one another. She knew what she enjoyed—alternative rock music (we shared a fondness for Modest Mouse, and she truly loved Radiohead), tacos (the Korean taco truck in Southern California and Chilango's in Providence), and casual, but colorful clothes (especially Lacoste sweaters). But she always adapted to the conditions of the moment, place, and personalities around her in order to maintain a constant balance. When discussions got too intense in the classroom, Tam offered a middle ground where different minds could, if not agree, at least debate without malice toward one another. When young activists were overwhelmed with passion or frustration, Tam provided counsel and instruction on how to move forward. She bridged cultures, often bringing together Latino, Asian, white, and black friends for activism, creating new friendships, and eating—always eating. And if the people around her ever forgot the primacy of love, she was there to gently remind us of the importance of being kind. Tam was simply the light and hope of the world for all who knew her, making her surroundings a more just, beautiful, and gentle place for all of us to live, think, and create.

> When young activists were **overwhelmed with passion** or frustration, Tam provided **counsel and instruction** on how to move forward

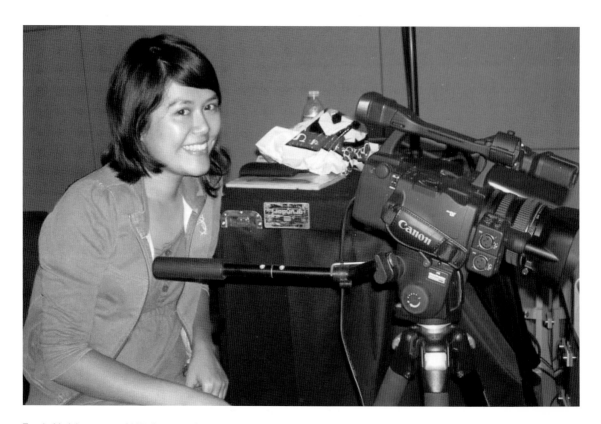

Tam behind the camera, 2007. *Courtesy of Eric Yao.*

breaking the silence:
remembering tam tran the scholar
Angela Chuan-Ru Chen and Tracy Lachica Buenavista

Tam Tran was a filmmaker, Dream activist, and doctoral student at Brown University. We also knew her as a friend, colleague, and emerging scholar. We were fortunate to spend our time with Tam eating, laughing, and talking about everything from relationships to family. We believe, however, that the space we created together was unique in that Tam often privately expressed to us perspectives that she rarely mentioned in public.

As one of the few Asian faces of the undocumented youth movement, Tam shared with us some of the misconceptions that fellow activists had about undocumented Asian youth, particularly their perceived silence. Her courageous activism made her a racial anomaly to most, but she knew she was not alone. From her own family's refugee experience, she understood that silence was not an inherent Asian characteristic, but rather a learned practice, conditioned by larger social, historical, and political contexts. Tam had a critical understanding of the complexities embedded in undocumented student experiences, and it was this aspect of her life that brought us together to collaborate on a project focused on undocumented Asian students.

The following is an excerpt from a manuscript that grew out of our collective desire to discuss the unique challenges facing undocumented Asian students. In this article based on a survey, we discuss the invisibility and perceived silence of undocumented Asian students. While Tam's insight flows throughout the article, this excerpt best highlights her work on the need to include and address Asian experiences in undocumented student discourse and to consider the intersection of race and immigration status to better understand undocumented student experiences. We feel especially fortunate to have captured her spirit and perspective in this essay and hope it provides a glimpse of the work for which Tam Tran the scholar strongly advocated.

Silence as a Sociocultural Practice

Under the model minority stereotype, Asian Americans are characterized as silent. Silence is racialized in that it often validates stereotypes of Asian Americans as simultaneously obedient, timid, and devious (Chou and Feagin 2008, 1, 39). In the context of undocumented students, a consistent assumption is made that Asian American issues remain unknown due to an inherent cultural value of nondisclosure. However, to understand Asian American silence, we must better consider the institutional forces that shape silence as a sociocultural practice. Further, we must acknowledge the instances in which undocumented Asian Americans have spoken out on undocumented student issues.

All of the survey respondents shared how they were considered "good" students. One Filipina student expressed, "The pressure of being the 'model minority' is very real, as most people don't even expect us to be 'troublemakers.'" Such a perception, in combination with the belief that undocumented Asian American students are quieter about their immigration status,

Tracy Buenavista, Tam, and Angela Chen at the Association of Asian American Studies Conference, 2009. *Courtesy of Angela Chen.*

affects the kind of resources that are available to Asian American students. One Mongolian student explained, "I think that Latino and Asian undocumented students face the same physical barriers, but we face completely different psychological and social barriers. Honestly, no one expects an Asian student to be undocumented, so we do not have the same kinds of resources as Latino students."

It is important to note that this statement was based on the student's previous efforts to seek resources. He experienced marginalization from those who were advocates for undocumented students. Students acknowledged that while the model minority assumption may initially seem positive in that it protects them from being labeled as undocumented, the stereotype prevents undocumented Asian American students from receiving the assistance they need from education practitioners.

In addition, undocumented Asian Americans identify how the need to protect themselves and their families by concealing their undocumented status is often misconstrued as silence predicated on Asian cultural values. The students acknowledge that there is a pattern of silence among undocumented Asian Americans but also challenge the notion that it is racially inherent and specific to Asian Americans. One Filipina student explained, "There is a social stigma with being undocumented. I didn't go around telling my friends because my mom always told us never to tell anyone outside of our immediate family." In general, undocumented status in the United States is not looked upon favorably. Undocumented people are perceived as criminal and socially and economically parasitic (Bernstein and Blazer 2008, 412–13). So undocumented people often do not disclose their status to people beyond their immediate families.

In the context of student experiences, scholars have highlighted how difficult it is for undocumented people to seek resources (Albrecht 2007, 193). Often the utilization of resources and services requires disclosure of basic information—name, address, citizenship status, social security number, etc. While collection of such information is considered mundane for most, undocumented people are subject to a certain level of vulnerability in revealing information that might indicate their undocumented status. The same student who previously described how her mother instructed her to be silent, analyzed her decision to do so: "Looking back, I see now that fear was a big part of what controlled my actions. Fear made me not ask for help or support from other people." As the policing of undocumented immigrants has increased, they are particularly susceptible to detention and deportation (Gorman 2009). Immigration and Customs Enforcement (ICE) raids have terrorized communities with particularly large segments of undocumented residents. Undocumented people are placed in danger

students, due to the complexity of her case as well as her academic accomplishments as a graduate from the University of California at Los Angeles and as a doctoral student at Brown University. Most notably, in May 2007, she testified in support of the DREAM Act before the House Judiciary Committee's Subcommittee on Immigration, Citizenship, Refugees, Border Security and International Law (Tran 2007).

Tran's experience contextualizes notions of Asian American silence in three ways. First, as the daughter of Vietnamese refugees, silence was a developed sociocultural practice for survival that emerged in the context of the Vietnam War. While Tran did not have direct contact with war, silence was a vestige of war present in the way her parents raised her. Second, although she

her courage to **speak on behalf** of other students demonstrates that silence is a **habit that can be broken**

by institutions, including colleges and universities, that do not provide protection for those without proper documentation.

While silence is considered necessary for survival, it is important to recognize the role that undocumented Asian Americans have played in informing the public about undocumented student issues. Tam Tran was a nationally recognized activist for undocumented student rights. The daughter of Vietnamese refugees, she was born in Germany and entered the United States as an adolescent. She remained stateless. A judge determined that it would be dangerous to deport her and her family to Vietnam, and Germany does not grant birthright citizenship and so will not accept her as a German resident. Tran has served as an important spokesperson for undocumented

notes the tendency for silence to pervade undocumented Asian American communities, her courage to speak on behalf of other students demonstrates that silence is a habit that can be broken and is often one imposed upon people with no legal rights in the United States. Finally, as silence is an imposed practice, the breaking of silence in an American militarized state can result in dire consequences. Following Tran's testimony, her family was arrested and detained by ICE agents, although they claimed their actions were independent of Tran's activism (Kiely 2007).

Silence poses a challenge for undocumented Asian American students because it is often mistaken as a marker to indicate that students do not need or want help. What is lacking in the analysis is how silence is coerced, learned, and conditioned, and not limited to Asian Americans. It is presumptuous to expect any undocumented student to display the same level of outspokenness as traditional students, and one must consider the consequences involved when undocumented students seek out educational assistance. Their silence does not indicate that undocumented Asian American students do not need or seek support.

References

Albrecht, Teri Jan. 2007. "Challenges and Service Needs of Undocumented Mexican Undergraduate Students: Students' Voices and Administrators' Perspectives." PhD diss., The University of Texas at Austin. http://proquest.umi.com/pqdlink?did=1441185871&Fmt=7&clientI%2d=79356&RQT=309&VName=PQD.

Bernstein, Josh, and Jonathan Blazer. 2008. "Legalizing Undocumented Immigrants: An Essential Tool in Fighting Poverty." *Journal of Poverty Law and Policy* 42, nos. 7–8: 408–15. http://www.nilc.org/document.html?id=63.

Chou, Rosalind S., and Joe R. Feagin. 2008. *The Myth of the Model Minority: Asian Americans Facing Racism.* Boulder, CO: Paradigm.

Gorman, Anna. 2009. "No Longer Rounding Up Just Fugitive Immigrants." *Los Angeles Times*, February 5.

Kiely, Kathy. 2007. "Immigrant's Family Detained after Daughter Speaks Out." *USA Today.* October 16. http://www.usatoday.com/news/washington/2007-10-16-Dream_N.htm.

Rincon, Alejandra. 2008. *Undocumented Immigrants and Higher Education: Si Se Puede.* New York: LFB Scholarly Publishing.

Tran, Tam. 2007. "Testimony of Tam Tran." Before the House Judiciary Committee's Subcommittee on Immigration, Citizenship, Refugees, Border Security and International Law. May 18. http://www.nilc.org/immlawpolicy/dream/tam-tran-2007-05-18.pdf.

Tam, *center*, with her family visiting France. *Courtesy of the Tran family.*

Tam and Cinthya take a break from filming *The Seattle Underground Railroad*, 2006. *Courtesy of the Felix family.*

Cinthya at Columbia University. *Courtesy of the Felix family.*

Cinthya and her family visit San Francisco, August 2009. *Courtesy of the Felix family.*

Tam and Cinthya take a break from filming *The Seattle Underground Railroad*, 2006. *Courtesy of the Felix family.*

Tam, age six, in the United States. *Courtesy of the Tran family.*

Although we mourn the passing of Cinthya and Tam,

we celebrate their lives

We won't tolerate hate!

Not in Los Angeles, not in California,
and **not in this country**.
Undocumented immigrants are
pushing back.

—Jonathan Perez, in front of Meg Whitman's office. In 2010 Whitman ran for governor of California on an anti-immigrant platform that threatened to make higher education inaccessible for undocumented students. *Courtesy of Erick Huerta*.

Part II

the immigrant
youth movement

What initially began as a campaign for the passage of the DREAM Act has transformed into a growing national movement led by immigrant youth. Dreamers, the beneficiaries of its passage, and their allies have taken the lead in galvanizing lawmakers and the larger community to support efforts to pass the DREAM Act.

Many versions of the DREAM Act have been debated since its introduction in 2001, but all contain core provisions offering eligible youth a path to citizenship upon the completion of higher education or service in the US military. The following reflections express the courage, passion, and strength of young leaders of this movement who are fighting for a dream.

"A Growing Movement." *Collage by May Kim.*

trail of dreams:
a fifteen-hundred-mile journey to the nation's capital

Gaby Pacheco

On July 26, 2006, ICE officers came to my house looking for me. They took my sister by mistake and took my parents and other sibling along with her. When ICE realized their mistake, I was told to come in right away or my family would be sent to different detention centers. I rushed to see my family where they were being detained and found my parents chained to chairs with handcuffs on their ankles. It was one of the most horrible days of my life. After a few difficult hours and an interrogation, ICE revealed that the reason they came looking for me was because I was speaking out to the media, and they did not like that. They let us all go but only after ordering me to stop talking to the media. However, I did not stay silent. I got involved in the immigrant rights movement because although I had a legal visa to remain in the United States, members of my family and many of my peers do not. It didn't seem fair that a small piece of paper gave me opportunities they didn't have.

I entered this country with a tourist visa, and my parents later obtained a student visa for me to study in the United States. When I graduated from fifth grade and went on to middle school, I lost that visa because my family didn't realize they had to reinstate it whenever I switched schools. This is how I learned about the importance of legal status in this country. When I graduated from high school, I was blessed to have found someone at Miami Dade College who helped me reinstate my visa again. The only way for me to maintain my status was to stay in school, paying international student rates and earning good grades. When I was asked to participate in the Trail of

The Trail of Dreams in Apopka, Florida, 2010. *Courtesy of Trail of Dreams.*

Dreams, I understood that it would mean making several sacrifices, including giving up my legal status because I would have to leave school. The importance of the Trail of Dreams overshadowed everything else, including a piece of paper that provided conditional status. This was an opportunity to fight for something bigger than myself.

On January 1, 2011, Felipe Matos, Carlos Roa, Juan Rodriguez, and I left Miami to embark on a fifteen-hundred-mile walk to our nation's capital. The Trail of Dreams was my way of challenging the distorted depiction of immigrants in this country. We set out to dispel the myths by talking to the average American. It was time to claim our

to take risks and lift our voices instead of settling for a life full of uncertainty. I have to remind myself that it is an oppressive, broken system that forces us to make these difficult and heartbreaking decisions.

From the very beginning when the participants talked about the Trail of Dreams, we knew we were going to engage in conversations with people from all walks of life. These included people who might have different beliefs or values from ours. We used nonviolent methods and had strategic conversations with people from across the political spectrum. On one occasion, we encountered a white, older US veteran who told us he strongly believed immigrants

When I was asked to participate in the **Trail of Dreams**, I understood that it would mean **giving up my legal status** because I would have to **leave school**

humanity and change people's hearts and minds by walking through our country one community at a time.

My decision triggered a lot of conflict within my family, and our attorneys were not happy with our decision. My family was concerned because I was the only one with legal status, and I was about to give it up. They said, "Why give up the little you have?" This made me reflect, and I concluded that the little I had was not worth much if it meant I had to stay silent as I watched other immigrant families get torn apart. This wasn't about me.

Every year my family wavers between feeling depressed and fighting to stay. My family received a final order to leave the country in 2009. Living in the shadows was safer, but because of my public fight, they now live in a dangerous light. I believe that being undocumented means we need

were destroying this country. He used hurtful words to describe us and even resorted to hurling slogans used by anti-immigrant groups to promote their views: "Illegal is illegal! What part of illegal don't you understand?" We let him speak his mind and tried to understand where he was coming from. He was a human being just like us and had a right to express himself. We wanted to make sure we listened before we shared our story.

After our conversation, he refrained from using the term "illegal" and used "undocumented" instead. He went on to wish us well, and we could tell that he genuinely hoped that we would be successful. This is an example of what we intended to do, to inform people about the immigration issue with the hope that they would see it from a humanitarian perspective. This encounter confirmed our belief that even

Members of the Trail of Dreams at a CNN interview, 2010. *Courtesy of Trail of Dreams.*

anti-immigrant extremists have hearts and minds and possess an ability to change. We were changing points of views one person at a time.

In Georgia we encountered members of the Ku Klux Klan (KKK) having a rally. There were people of all ages surrounded by large Confederate flags. We watched as frail senior citizens were helped into their white robes and hoods and saw parents placing small robes on their children. It was a surreal display of the steadfast, racist views of a small subculture. We decided to have a protest with thirty of our supporters to share our point of view with the crowd gathered on the other side of the street.

The two groups faced each other with police separating us to prevent any incidents. The other walkers and I decided to talk to those attending the KKK rally to have a conversation about our issues. We discovered that there were three types of people at the KKK rally: those who were in strong agreement with the KKK, those who were curious about what the KKK had to say, and those who were angry that the rally was happening in their community. Not everyone expressed hateful resentment toward us, and we engaged in some meaningful, productive conversations, which was in direct opposition to the behavior the KKK members were inciting at their rally.

Unfortunately, racist, anti-immigrant groups like the KKK are gaining momentum all across the South. The human rights of many immigrants are violated each day in this country. We need systemic change that spreads beyond legislative battles down to each individual who can make change.

Throughout our walk, we learned how beautiful the human spirit is. We were joined by immigrant day laborers and their families. Even though they told us they had not been able to find work for weeks or months, they donated dimes, nickels, and pennies so that we could continue our trip. They walked with us and helped us carry our backpacks for the time they were with us. We stopped at dozens of places along the way, with growing support as we crossed each state line. Through all of our challenges, we were also welcomed with open arms. At certain points, thousands were walking with us, sometimes a dozen, and sometimes the four of us walked alone. Solidarity walks were concurrently organized across the country. We arrived in Washington, DC, on May 1, 2010, a day when immigrant rights marches took place across the country. The Trail of Dreams walkers carried with us the voices of struggle and hope from families we met along the way, creating change one step at a time.

following the civil rights trail:
my pilgrimage to the south

Renata Teodoro

I was born in Brazil. My parents were very poor growing up and never went to high school because they had to work to help sustain their families. After my two siblings and I were born, my dad had a hard time finding a job, so he went to the United States to work and support us. It was hard on all of us to have our family separated.

I was six years old when my mom told me we were going to the United States, and I started crying. I did not want to leave my grandparents or my friends. When my mother told me Mickey Mouse lived in the United States, I was more compliant. It was my childhood dream to see jubilant Disney cartoon characters and have happily-ever-after endings. After years of not seeing my father, we were finally reunited

as a family, and that is all that mattered. We never made it to Disneyland, and our life wasn't a Disney cartoon that ended happily ever after. We lived with my uncle and his wife in Duluth, Minnesota, and we rarely got to see our parents because they were always at work. They worked hard, and we were struggling to survive. I remember one time my father sold his own blood just so he could put food on the table.

During these hard times, my mom asked me if I liked living in the United States, and I said no. Then she asked me if I wanted to leave, and I also said no. It was a confusing time for me. While life was hard here, it also seemed daunting to go back. We crossed many borders to get here, and I was afraid of the journey back. She

Renata Teodoro, *standing*, joins members of SIM outside the Massachusetts State House, 2010. *Courtesy of Josh Savala.*

then said something I will never forget. She explained that the reason it was so difficult for us to travel to the United States but so easy to go back to Brazil was because "we weren't supposed to be here."

We eventually moved to Massachusetts, where my parents started their own business and bought a house. Things were improving, but I was always apprehensive about someone finding out that we "weren't supposed to be here." I poured all my energy into doing well in school and making friends. I tried my best to forget and hoped that if I just kept quiet, one day things would change.

During middle school, I started researching immigration issues and found out about different proposed bills that could possibly help me. I thought that by the time I got to high school, the DREAM Act or immigration reform would have passed. In the meantime, I learned how to survive as an undocumented student by working in the underground economy and occasionally driving without a license.

But my family situation got complicated. My father abandoned us and went back to Brazil. We had to sell our house and move into a smaller house in Brockton, Massachusetts, but we didn't let that disrupt our bond as a family. We worked together to make that house our new home.

Senior year of high school came, and I was still in the same situation. One day I was called out of my classroom and asked to go to the school auditorium. I was surrounded by my friends and classmates who were waiting for me, and I found out that I had won a prestigious scholarship. The scholarship would pay for my educational fees all through college. I was really excited. But my heart sank when I read the requirements, one of which was a social security number. While everyone else was celebrating, I wanted to cry as I sat through the long ceremony.

I decided that no one would stop me from going to a university. I took all the money that I had saved from working throughout high school and used it to pay tuition at the University of Massachusetts, Boston. My first semester was amazing, and I felt privileged to be there.

However, during a break from school, ICE officers came to my house. My younger sister and my brother's girlfriend were the

SIM members with Dr. Terrence Roberts, *left*, of the Little Rock Nine. *Courtesy of SIM.*

They taught me that **students** from the Civil Rights Movement were **similar to us**—uncertain and sometimes afraid—but that did not stop them from **standing up and fighting**

only ones home. They didn't know it was ICE, so they called my brother to come home. As soon as he stepped out of his car, they handcuffed him. He had just left his construction job, and he was still in his dirty clothes. My mother and I got a call and rushed home. We found that they had searched our house and told my little sister they would be back for the rest of us.

That night I remember feeling like a prisoner in my own home. My mom told us that we needed to go back to Brazil because she would not be able to live with herself if another one of her children ended up in handcuffs. That's when I made the decision that I would stay. My mom was angry at me, but she respected my decision. She ended up sending my little sister back to Brazil. My brother was eventually released, but he also had to go back to Brazil. My mother turned herself in to ICE and was also sent away. I was the only one in my family who stayed behind.

When I was beginning to lose hope, I found an organization called Student Immigrant Movement (SIM) on Facebook. It was the first organization I had ever heard of with undocumented students leading campaigns for immigration reform. I quickly became involved in the fight for the DREAM Act. In late 2009, SIM embarked on a pilgrimage to the South. We wanted to gain a deeper understanding of how our experiences as undocumented immigrant students compared to the struggles of African American students during the Civil Rights Movement. The Civil Rights

Movement was a source of inspiration to us, and we wanted to learn about the brave students who changed the hearts and minds of millions.

Our first stop was Clinton, Tennessee, where we hoped to meet members of the Clinton Twelve, the first group of African American students to desegregate an all-white high school in the South in 1956. Prior to the Civil Rights Movement, blacks were forced to go to segregated and usually inferior schools. These students were being denied access to equal education because of the color of their skin. Their simple desire to attend high school caused many people to react with anger and violence. Still, they stood strong and fought against hatred and ignorance to pursue their education.

We arrived at the Green McAdoo Cultural Center where we met Jerry Shattuck, who serves on the board of the museum. He showed us an exhibit on the story of the Clinton Twelve. We sat in their desks, read the hate mail they received, and viewed photographs of their school. Their school was bombed in 1958, and we saw photographs of the devastation.

Jerry Shattuck later revealed that he had attended high school with the Clinton Twelve and even protected them during those years as a white student ally. He said, "I am a law-abiding citizen, and that was the law at the time, so I was going to do everything I could to follow it." The statement made me wonder how he would react to our situation, as people who do not hold legal status in this country. I was very nervous, but I decided to share my story with Jerry. To our shock and excitement, Jerry was inspired by the reasons we were there, and he offered to call members of the Clinton Twelve, meet with us. Thanks to Jerry's call, we met two amazing people, Anna Theresser Caswell and Maurice Soles. They were incredibly humble, but the magnitude of their actions resonates deeply with us today, just as it did throughout the South over fifty years ago. They were supportive of our cause and wished us well.

We left Tennessee in good spirits and headed to Arkansas, where we met Dr. Terrence Roberts and Carlotta Walls Lanier, two members of the Little Rock Nine. In 1957 the Little Rock Nine were African American students who were physically denied entrance by the Arkansas National Guard when they attempted to attend the segregated Little Rock Central High School. They were followed by a mob who threatened to lynch them. It was not until President Eisenhower sent the United States Army to protect them that they were able to attend a previously all-white high school.

Dr. Roberts and Ms. Lanier listened to our stories as undocumented students and asked many questions. They offered their thoughts on the issue, and we drew important parallels between our movements. I learned how both our struggles were about access to education and racial equity. I also understood that our issues were intimately connected and rooted firmly in US history, in the ways American society has marginalized people of color and immigrants. Only through our common struggles have we been able to combat institutions that support racism and unequal access to education.

I gained much inspiration and support from the words of the Clinton Twelve and the Little Rock Nine. They taught me that students from the Civil Rights Movement were similar to us—uncertain and sometimes afraid—but that did not stop them from standing up and fighting. Ultimately we all seek ways to humanize our issues and claim our right to exist. I knew from that moment on, I had to put my fear aside and toil on.

the dream graduation

Matias Ramos

Graduation ceremonies celebrate the uniformity of the graduating class, marching in identical caps and gowns to signify a completed regimen of coursework. The Dream Graduation is a form of street theater performed by undocumented students as early as 2003. These mock graduations symbolize the desire of undocumented students to fully belong to that educational world and provide a visual representation of the diversity of the immigrant youth movement.

I especially remember a mock graduation that took place in California in 2007. I marched with fellow immigrant youth through the streets of downtown Los Angeles for an event organized by the California Dream Network, a statewide network of college student organizations who work on undocumented student issues. We came together from different colleges and donned graduation caps from different high schools, and though we did not know one another well, we performed collectively for what we saw as the cause of our lives. There was not only beauty in the multicolored gowns but also power in combining the symbols of graduation with direct action, such as closing down afternoon traffic in a city obsessed with traffic.

In 2009 United We Dream and other organizations called for mock graduations to be organized across the country to mobilize support for the DREAM Act. This was an early attempt at national organizing and strategic alliance building led by

Matias Ramos leads a chant at a Dream Graduation, 2007. *Courtesy of Horacio Arroyo.*

undocumented students. Integrating a press conference as part of the ceremonial rally provided the opportunity to bring together mass action by undocumented students and vocal support from public advocates. Undocumented students were able to take a public stand and see themselves as part of a large contingent of young people advocating for social change. Members of Congress, as well as supporters representing labor, business, education, and faith-based public interest groups, articulated the many reasons to support the DREAM Act. This public testimony became a fundamental political tool for the movement.

High-school graduation has remained an elusive goal for many undocumented young people living in the United States.

According to a report by the Migration Policy Institute, around 489,000 undocumented people between the ages of eighteen and thirty-four do not have a high school diploma or GED (Batalova and McHugh 2010), rendering them ineligible to start the legalization process that the DREAM Act would provide. However, as a movement, we continue to reach out to young people in high school and encourage them to pursue their dreams through higher education.

In our dream graduations, we celebrate our differences and more importantly our aspirations. The first decade of the century saw the birth of undocumented youth activism; may the next decade propel us to victory.

Reference

Batalova, Jeanne, and Margie McHugh. 2010. "DREAM vs. Reality: An Analysis of Potential DREAM Act Beneficiaries." Migration Policy Institute, *Insight*, July. http://www.migrationpolicy.org/pubs /DREAM-Insight-July2010.pdf.

Undocumented students were able to **take a public stand** and see themselves as part of a large contingent of young people **advocating for social change**

coming out of the shadows

Ireri Unzueta

I moved to the United States with my parents and sister in 1994, just as I was turning seven years old. At that time, my world consisted of my toys—especially my marbles—and the love of my family. I did not understand how difficult it was for my parents to leave our home in Mexico and come to a new country. I wasn't fully aware of my family's financial struggles or of how ill I had become from the pollution near our home.

My mother tried very hard to create a home for us here. She enrolled me in several after-school activities, so I would not have time to miss the family we left behind. She decorated my room because I never put any effort into making it mine. My mother kept the house filled with music, made sure that we sat down for meals as a family, and planned family field trips to museums. And so the four of us, far away from anyone we knew, attempted to form new lives here.

For many of the years I lived in this country, I refused to let myself feel at home. That feeling began my first summer in the United States when kids in the playground refused to speak Spanish with me, even though they clearly understood me. It took me about twelve years to adjust; twelve years of making friends and creating an extended family; twelve years of learning a new culture through TV shows, alternative music, and by joining different groups at school and in the community; twelve years during which my inner language shifted from Spanish to English.

Ireri Unzueta publicly declares her status in Chicago, March 2010. *Courtesy of Peter Holderness.*

One day in 2007 after spending a few days away, I remember feeling like I could not wait to get home to continue my work with the art collective I had joined. I finally felt a sense of belonging. But this was not reciprocated by the outside world, at least not by the legal system and the authorities. This was particularly apparent when my sister and I began to navigate the educational system.

When my sister was ready for college, she returned to Mexico to apply for a student visa to allow her to attend college in this country. Her petition was denied, and she was stuck in Mexico. My parents

do with my life. Legally I cannot work but out of necessity, I do what I can by finding temporary jobs that pay under the table. I wrestle with the thought of investing time in pursuing a career that could become my passion, but I would have to lie about my legal status to do it. For the same reason, I never considered the health care field, which would have been my chosen career. What if in the end I can't find a career?

By the end of 2009, I grew frustrated at how the avenues I wanted to pursue seemed closed off. Around that time, I also began to meet other young undocumented people who were just as frustrated

It has become clear to me that

deportations will continue to

happen until we all

come out of the shadows

embarked on a public campaign to bring her back to the United States, and she was finally able to come back conditionally. When I was in high school thinking about college, I found out how frustrating it is to sit and look through piles of scholarships and only be able to apply to two or three because of my lack of legal status, despite my qualifications. Something was definitely not right.

I was eventually able to attend a university and luckily had parts of my tuition covered by a variety of scholarships from my school. Occasionally I attended a study-abroad information session, playing with the idea of applying and dealing with the legal consequences of traveling later. Studying abroad seemed like the quintessential college experience. But I knew that it would not be possible, at least if I wanted to remain in the United States with my family.

I graduated with a bachelor of arts degree in 2009. This made my mother happy, but I was at a loss as to what to

and angry and who, like me, felt that this country was their home. We were not going to remain silent. One of these young people was actually in deportation proceedings, and it made me more aware and critical of the arbitrary immigration enforcement policies carried out by ICE. This pushed me to break my silence and publicly declare my immigration status.

The Immigrant Youth Justice League of Chicago held the National Coming Out of the Shadows Day on March 10, 2010. About a thousand participants marched from Union Park to Federal Plaza, where the event ended with a rally. My sister and I were among the group of eight activists who publicly announced our immigration status in our speeches. This action was the first of its kind in the nation and for the rest of the month, similar actions across the country followed. We finally lost the fear of talking about our long-kept secret: we are undocumented. We had realized the power of speaking about our experiences in public and using our voices to sway opinions and counter the toxic anti-immigrant rhetoric that has flooded our country.

I was not afraid that day even with rumors floating around that ICE officers would be showing up at our demonstration. I could not stand by anymore and watch our dreams get pushed aside and see our families suffer. I was tired of hearing about immigration raids conducted in the middle of the night when no one would notice. I took notice. The people who came out that day with me took notice.

After we shared our stories, we marched with hundreds of other undocumented youth and allies through the streets of downtown Chicago embracing our new identity. We started by shouting, "No papers, no fear, immigrants are marching here!" And then alongside hundreds of people, we finally chanted loudly and proudly,

"Undocumented and Unafraid! Undocumented and Unafraid!" Since then, we have carried the same slogan on our signs, in our hearts, and in our minds.

I have participated in various acts of civil disobedience—my sister was one of the first undocumented students in the country to participate in this kind of direct action—and I have yet to be placed in deportation proceedings. On the other hand, I hear about young people getting deported every day. The only difference is that we made our stories public and have worked to build community support. It has become clear to me that deportations will continue to happen until we all come out of the shadows. My message to the government and to those who still think we will silently stand by: we are paying attention, we are losing our fear, and we are not giving up.

Tania Unzueta at a rally in Chicago, March 2010. *Courtesy of Peter Holderness.*

the mccain five:
dream act students submit to arrest for the first time in history

Lizbeth Mateo, Mohammad Abdollahi, Yahaira Carrillo, Tania Unzueta, and Raúl Alcaraz

Senator John McCain of Arizona was a cosponsor of the DREAM Act in 2007. He was also running for president of the United States. Minutes before the DREAM Act was scheduled for a vote, McCain left the Senate chambers to avoid casting a vote. McCain had been a leader of bipartisan immigration reform and was a staunch supporter of the DREAM Act. But his presidential ambitions led him to betray the students he had pledged to support in order to court anti-immigrant Republican voters.

For ten years, Congress has failed time and time again to pass legislation that would provide a pathway to citizenship for undocumented immigrant students, and they keep telling us that we have to wait. We chose to take action because we knew we could no longer allow government leaders and mainstream immigrant rights advocates to dictate the course of our movement.

On May 17, 2010, on the fifty-sixth anniversary of *Brown v. Board of Education*, four undocumented students—Lizbeth Mateo, Mohammad Abdollahi, Yahaira Carrillo, and Tania Unzueta, along with one ally, Raúl Alcaraz—became the first youth to risk deportation by staging a sit-in inside Senator McCain's office in Tucson, Arizona, to demand the immediate passage of the DREAM Act. We wanted to tell him that when he walked out on the DREAM Act vote in 2007, he undermined the futures of thousands of young people. We wanted to show Senator McCain—who acted as a coward—the face of courage.

Lizbeth Mateo's family came to this country when she was fourteen years old from Oaxaca, Mexico. In Oaxaca, her father

Tania, Lizbeth, Yahaira, Mohammad, and Raul sit inside the office of Senator McCain. *Courtesy of Anselmo Rascón.*

was a taxicab driver, while her mother took care of the children at home. Her parents struggled to make ends meet, but they were faced with the choice between seeing their children get sick and starve or risking it all by coming to the United States. Lizbeth's life has been full of uncertainty and tough choices, but she became the first in her family to graduate from high school and from college. She dreams of becoming a lawyer one day and defending the cause of liberty and justice before the US Supreme Court.

Mohammad Abdollahi, originally from Iran, developed a community with other undocumented students online. He first found out about his immigration status in middle school but did not know the implications of his situation, because his parents never discussed it. When Mohammad

the situation and its members' actions. The attention we generated in the national press prevented ICE from aggressively moving to deport us. This doesn't mean we are safe, but it does reflect the contradictions within the broken immigration system. Undocumented immigrants across the country face harsh conditions every day and live in the shadows, in fear of being detained by ICE when they drive a car, take the train, or go to work. As DREAM-Act-eligible youth, we recognize the advantages we have as educated young people who have the capacity to organize and resist oppression.

The goal of our sit-in in McCain's office was simple: to push for the DREAM Act as a stand-alone bill. Some immigrant rights advocates only supported comprehensive immigration reform and worked to block

We knew in our hearts that **deportation was a risk** we were willing to take

graduated from high school and applied to community college, he realized his immigration status was going to be a challenge. He worked full time and took night classes to continue his education. He tried to transfer to a university but was denied access when they realized he was undocumented. When he met other undocumented students online, he became an activist and began to connect with other activists across the country. He was one of the founders of Dreamactivist.org, a web site that has become central to the work of the movement. Mohammad is gay and would face prison, or worse, if he were returned to Iran. Mohammad risked it all in order to fight for immigrant rights in the country he calls home.

The McCain Five are part of an organizing movement that must constantly evaluate

the DREAM Act from moving forward. Our objective was to use this act of civil disobedience to change that. We expected to be detained for weeks for our actions and possibly face deportation proceedings, during which time our supporters would push as hard as they could for the passage of the DREAM Act.

Prior to the civil disobedience, we spent a week in Washington, DC, talking to various Senate offices to encourage them to move the DREAM Act, because we knew that immigrant youth across the country were ready to mobilize on the ground. We also met with an immigration attorney who promised to represent us in court. Locally we activated all of our allies, including immigrant youth groups and community based organizations, to put pressure on Congress. In spite of our growing movement,

Congress was unable to find the courage to pass the DREAM Act in 2010. They were unable to honestly reflect on the history of our country and its immigrant foundations.

Three of us (Yahaira, Mohammad, and Lizbeth) were arrested and turned over to ICE, while wearing our graduation caps and gowns. We knew in our hearts that deportation was a risk we were willing to take and that even if we were deported, we would leave knowing that we fought until the end, giving everything we possibly could to make our dream a reality. These are the choices immigrant youth must make. Following our action, many other undocumented youth have taken the same steps. We will continue to fight until we prevail in the halls of Congress.

"Free Dream Act 5," 2010.
Design by Raymundo M. Hernández-López, MA (Aryer).

the wilshire nine:
stopping traffic and fighting for our dreams

Nancy Meza

On May 20, 2010, nine brave students sat down in the middle of Wilshire Boulevard in front of the West Los Angeles Federal Building to advocate for passage of the DREAM Act. The Wilshire Nine action took place three days after DREAM Act students staged a sit-in at Senator McCain's office in Arizona. In Los Angeles, immigrant youth came together to take part in a similar nonviolent direct action. Direct action disrupts "business as usual" but most importantly, it is an act of sacrifice by individuals who are willing to put themselves at risk in order to push for the greater good.

The nine demonstrators were all US citizens, but they took this action in solidarity with their undocumented friends and classmates. One of the protestors was an Iraq War veteran. We chose Wilshire Boulevard because it is one of the busiest thoroughfares in Los Angeles and is located a few blocks from UCLA. Dozens of supporters marched in a picket line surrounding the Wilshire Nine, who took over the street for two hours, sitting in a circle wearing graduation caps.

I was stationed with my laptop computer and cell phone a few blocks away at a coffee shop, conducting media outreach for the action. The coffee shop was our makeshift office, and I sent out press releases with updates and took calls from many reporters. I was identified as the media spokesperson on the press release, and my cell phone number was listed.

The traffic congestion caused by the street closure was immense. Television and radio reporting of traffic delays is a constant preoccupation in Los Angeles, so a traffic jam caused by civil disobedience attracted considerable media coverage. Little did we know that one of the motorists stranded in

Sit-in in front of the Federal Building near UCLA, May 2010. *Courtesy of Jonathan Bibriesca.*

traffic was a right-wing talk radio host who regularly spews anti-immigrant rhetoric on his shows.

As I was conducting an interview for an international cable news show, my phone began to ring repeatedly. I answered a few calls and was attacked and insulted. One caller told me, "You need to understand that illegal is illegal," whereas another voiced that "illegals like you need to be deported back to Mexico." I soon learned that a national campaign had been started by the conservative AM radio talk show to call for my deportation.

I was unaware of the radio show's reach and was shocked to discover its popularity. I listened to the radio broadcast and was disgusted by the distorted information sent out to its listeners. The sacrifice that our allies made in order to push for the passage of the DREAM Act was being used to demonize immigrant youth.

the thought of parents' buying "Deport Nancy Meza" t-shirts for their children and babies to wear.

I came to the United States from Mexico at the age of two and have been living here as an undocumented immigrant for more than twenty years. I grew up in the poor, working-class neighborhood of East Los Angeles and was the first person in my family to graduate from high school and go on to college. Although I had experienced various instances of anti-immigrant sentiment, this attack was the worst by far. Nevertheless, it has made me stronger and prouder to be undocumented and unafraid.

As undocumented students, we have decided that while we take a risk in exposing ourselves and revealing our undocumented status, the greater risk is when we remain silent and unknown to the world around us. Although exposing myself as an undocumented student sparked a

I soon learned that a **national campaign** had been started by the conservative AM radio talk show **to call for my deportation**

That day I received hundreds of hateful and racist calls, text messages, and e-mails. However, I also received messages of love and support from friends, classmates, and professors who were shocked that right-wing talk shows had launched a national campaign calling for my deportation. The shows also announced on the air that they were selling a printed t-shirt advertised online as part of the campaign. "Deport Nancy Meza" was printed on the front of the shirt, with a phone number for Immigration and Customs Enforcement on the back. It was available in different colors and sizes for about thirty dollars and even included baby and toddler sizes. I couldn't fathom

national call for my deportation, that same act informed and mobilized my community and other supporters about the realities we face and motivated them to take action. I have not faced deportation, but it is a risk that I am willing to take for justice. I know this risk might result in being torn away from my family and sent to a place I have not seen since I was two years old, but this is the reality that far too many immigrants face. It is a reality that needs to be changed. If I can do anything to advance the fight for human dignity and justice, I will do so, even if it means being separated from my family and loved ones.

dream freedom ride

Cyndi Bendezu

On July 9, 2010, twelve undocumented students and allies embarked on a journey that changed our lives. The Dream Freedom Ride was inspired by the 1961 Freedom Rides, when young black and white civil rights activists traveled to the South to challenge segregation and Jim Crow laws. The Freedom Riders defied the status quo and emerged as a voice of conscience in opposition to racism and racial exclusion. The riders demonstrated incredible courage, facing the KKK, lynch mobs, and state-sanctioned violence throughout the South. Their spirit encouraged a group of immigrant youth to drive in rented vans across the country, risking legal persecution and the threat of deportation, especially in states with staunch anti-immigrant policies.

Our plan was to lobby in key states, engage in direct action, and publicize our campaign for the DREAM Act. We arranged to connect with various faith-based, labor, youth, and immigrant rights groups in each state along the way and to meet with key Senate leadership to urge them to pass the DREAM Act as a stand-alone bill. Throughout the year, many immigrant rights organizations had been promoting the DREAM Act only as an attachment to a comprehensive immigration reform bill. However, immigrant youth throughout the country decided to create our own strategy of calling for the DREAM Act as a stand-alone bill. Given the political realities in Congress, we felt that the DREAM Act had an opportunity to pass if it were introduced separately.

Our drive began at the UCLA Downtown Labor Center, which served as our base of operation. The first stop was in Las Vegas, Nevada, where we had scheduled a meeting with the staff of US Senate Majority Leader Harry Reid. However, we were not allowed inside the federal building because some

Logo design by Xavi Moreno, 2010.

of us did not have government issued IDs. Instead, we were forced to meet outside in the 102-degree heat. From that point in the trip forward, we decided that we would never be divided as a group when it came to questions about our legal status.

Our time in Arizona was the most intimidating, particularly because fierce anti-immigrant policies had recently been implemented by the state legislature and governor. Arizona's Senate Bill 1070, which criminalizes immigrants, could have been used against our undocumented riders. Thankfully we made it out of Arizona to Utah, where we visited the offices of Republican Senators Bob Bennet and Orrin Hatch. Their Cedar City, Utah, offices were nothing more than storage rooms with answering machines, so we were unable to meet with staff members to advocate for our cause. We then travelled to Denver, Colorado, where we had a successful press conference with Padres y Jovenes Unidos, a local immigrant rights organization.

In Nebraska, we visited the offices of Democratic Senator Ben Nelson and Republican Senator Mike Johanns, both of whom have opposed the DREAM Act. After those lobbying visits, we had a press conference outside the capitol building with Appleseed Nebraska, one of the few community-based immigrant rights organizations in the region. We then went back on the road to Illinois, where we participated in a press conference in Chicago with the Immigrant Youth Justice League, who were joining us on their way to Washington, DC.

When we arrived in DC, we joined immigrant youth from around the country in a civil disobedience action in the halls of Congress. Twenty-one courageous undocumented immigrant youth, wearing caps and gowns, were arrested inside the Capitol building. One of our own riders, Laura Lopez, was arrested in the office of Senator Harry Reid. She was later released and joined us on our journey home.

Throughout our trip, we received support and encouragement from complete strangers who learned about our cause and stepped forward to help us. They provided food, places to rest, and money for gas. They reached out to their friends and networks and helped us organize educational events along the way. We developed relationships with labor, community, legal, student, and faith-based groups and built support for our movement. We also came to realize that we are fighting for more than just a piece of legislation; we are fighting for our lives. And our fight will not end until we win education, justice, and freedom for all.

Their **spirit encouraged**
a group of immigrant youth to drive in
rented vans across the country,
risking legal persecution
and the threat of deportation

Community fund-raiser for the Dream Freedom Ride, 2010. *Courtesy of Patricia Torres.*

civil disobedience in washington, dc
Laura Lopez

I was twenty months old when my mom and I left Mexico in 1989 to reunite with my dad, who was already residing in the United States. Once we were here, my parents filed a claim for asylum. Their asylum petition was denied, and they were immediately placed in removal proceedings. They filed to stop their deportation, and a judge remained undecided on whether or not to deport them.

My parents struggled with the immigration system for over ten years while they tried to raise a family. My US-born sister had a rare form of rickets and needed

"I Exist!" Illustration by Julio Salgado.

my parents to care for her. After years of uncertainty, the judge decided to stop their deportation. The chance my parents took by coming out of the shadows and petitioning to stay in the United States changed our lives forever. My parents are now legal permanent residents and are eligible for US citizenship. I also have four younger US-born siblings who are all citizens. This may sound like a story of how the immigration system can work to help keep families together, but one person from our family was left out. I am still undocumented.

As soon as my parents were granted residency in 2004, my father filed a petition for me. We were told that the United States Citizenship and Immigration Services was processing the applications filed in 1992 for "sons or daughters over 21 of Legal Permanent Residents from Mexico." Even after my application is reviewed, I could still face a ten-year bar from the United States because I have been living here—the only home I have ever known—without authorization. So I may have to wait until I am over forty years old to finally attain legal status. There is no question about it, our immigration system is broken. I decided to do something about it.

On July 20, 2010, I was arrested in Washington, DC, as part of a nonviolent civil disobedience action in support of the passage of the DREAM Act, a piece of legislation that could have helped me and thousands of other students like me. While thirteen students were arrested in the lobby of the Senate building, eight of us sat in key Senate offices to urge congressional leadership to take action and pass the DREAM Act. After two months of coast-to-coast actions, we were ready to bring the cause of our lives to our nation's capital. The immigrant youth who participated in this action came from Illinois, Virginia, New York, California, Arizona, Kansas, Missouri, and Michigan. Prior to this day, I had never been arrested. Just like my parents, I came out of the shadows and took a chance by risking it all for a better future. I also

Another member's mother had passed away a few years ago; for him, the sit-in was to honor his mother's risk when she crossed the border and to gain the opportunity to go to college. These stories touched us. Our parents always want us to have better lives than they had, which is why they migrated and why we are here.

While listening to these stories and asking the Senate staff about their own children, I reflected on my generation and

Our parents always want us to **have better lives** than they had, which is why they migrated and **why we are here**

wanted to protest the harsh immigration laws that could separate me from my family.

The day I sat in a Senator's office, I was filled with feelings of sorrow. I had prepared myself to be arrested, to sit in a jail cell, and to make a single phone call. As part of the larger movement, we had all prepared for months for the possible consequences. But this action gave me the opportunity to fully reflect on what was at stake. We had to risk arrest to remain in the United States. We wanted real change to happen. We were tired of the grand speeches and cold compromises that often gamble with the lives of immigrants. Immigration reform is not just about changing the regulations about who can cross what border; it's about allowing families to stay together and live in dignity.

Many of us had lobbied our own representatives to cosponsor or vote for the DREAM Act. But that day, it became personal. Most dreamers came to this country accompanying our brave parents on a plane, in a car, or wading across a river. The day of the sit-in, we shared stories of the family ties that kept us here. One member had an ailing mother; he participated in the sit-in to show his mother, while she was still alive, that she had succeeded in raising him well and giving him a better life.

the generation that is to come. A student from my group, Isabel Castillo, asked two congressional staff members a question that resonated deeply within me: "Wouldn't you do anything for your child to have a better life, even take them to another country?" They both answered yes.

For the first time I realized that even without the passage of any type of immigration reform, life would still go on. I am getting older, and I am going through the adult rites of passage regardless of my status. I graduated from the University of California, Santa Cruz, with honors. With the DREAM Act or without the DREAM Act, I plan to go to law school. But I have decided that without legal status, I will not become a parent. I will not raise my child with the constant fear of separation due to our broken immigration system. I am not willing to raise a child in a society that will punish him or her for having an undocumented mother. I cannot imagine my child telling anyone, "People came and took my mom." While this is a painful decision, I continue to have faith that things will change. Meanwhile, I will keep fighting for my future by taking risks and challenging inhumane laws that separate families.

dream university

Maricela Aguilar

During the summer of 2010, United We Dream (UWD) launched Dream University, a series of public teach-ins in Washington, DC. "If they don't let us go to school, we will build our own," was the slogan embraced by Dream University. The first educational program was held on July 14, 2010, in Lafayette Park, a public area in front of the White House. At the time, there were three Dream organizers working on the project. I was the "admissions director" and began to recruit youth organizations from across the country to come to DC. I arranged everything from logistics to programming. We

Students march in Washington, DC, 2010.
Courtesy of Fabiola Inzunza.

hoped to establish an environment reflecting the principle that the right to higher education belongs to everyone, regardless of nationality, race, or immigration status.

Things began falling into place as more organizers joined us in time for the arrival of our Dream University students. They came from as far away as Florida (Students Working for Equal Rights), Wisconsin (Youth Empowered in the Struggle), and the heartland (Kansas/Missouri Dream Alliance). Dream University was hectic. We were sleep-deprived, enduring extreme heat, and always under the watchful eye of the park police. On our second day, we were kicked out of the park because we lacked the proper permits. We were forced to sit on the hot asphalt in between Lafayette Park and the White House, the only nearby space that was completely public property. There was a heat warning that day and absolutely no shade, but all of our students sat down without complaint and attended class. Thankfully we were able to obtain a permit the next day and continue our classes on the shady grounds of Lafayette Park.

Over the next few weeks, hundreds of undocumented students came to chant, dance, teach, and learn, while we fought for the DREAM Act. Professors, advocates, and young leaders from the region served as guest lecturers, sharing their insight into topics as varied as American history, legal studies, and organizing theory. We were also able to educate many of DC's tourists about our campaign.

Dream University was the first national event I had ever organized. Previously

I had only organized local events in my hometown of Milwaukee, Wisconsin, with Youth Empowered in the Struggle (YES!), which is part of the larger umbrella organization, Voces de la Frontera. YES took on a campaign for in-state tuition rates for undocumented students. As an undocumented student, it was empowering to learn basic organizing, and I went public as an undocumented student for the first time at a YES coming-out rally.

Through my organizing, I learned about the daunting challenges facing other undocumented students. In some ways, I was privileged to have grown up with my entire family together, and I received a full tuition scholarship to one of the top private universities in my state. But I realized that opportunities like the one I had should be made available to everyone. Although I am still undocumented and face other barriers, I began to see our fight as part of the broader struggle for fundamental change in our communities and to ensure equal access to education for all.

Those of us in the struggle are living, breathing proof that change is possible, but the problem with change is that it takes a very long time. Organizers often reach a point of complete exhaustion. But that was never the case with Dream University. We knew that our efforts were going to make our nation better for generations to come, and this filled us with energy. Although we might not be able to see all the fruits of our labor, we planted some seeds of change. The purpose of Dream University was to inspire undocumented youth across the country and build momentum for a national Dream Graduation. We also supported the first civil disobedience action by undocumented students in the halls of Congress.

Dream University contributed to our growing movement because we ourselves created the change we needed in our lives. We hope to ensure quality education for all students, for those who participated in Dream University, and for many more who have yet to discover the power of their identity and struggle.

If they don't let us go to school,
we will build our own

Logo design by Remeike Forbes.

fasting for our dream:
nationwide hunger strikes push for the passage of the dream act

Carlos Amador

Banner in front of Senator Dianne Feinstein's Los Angeles office, summer 2010. *Courtesy of Adrian Gonzalez.*

While twenty-one undocumented immigrant youth were risking deportation by staging a civil disobedience action in the halls of Congress on July 20, 2010, a group of Southern California student activists were inspired to escalate our movement. The following day, I joined eight other undocumented students and allies from Dream Team Los Angeles, Orange County Dream Team, and other local groups to begin a hunger strike outside of the Los Angeles office of US Senator Diane Feinstein. Following the traditions of Mahatma Gandhi and César Chávez, we chose to engage in an act of nonviolence and sacrifice. Our goal was to urge Senator Feinstein, a supporter of the DREAM Act and member of the Senate Judiciary Committee, to move the DREAM Act to the Senate floor. The stalemate in Congress over immigration reform and the DREAM Act continued to leave thousands of undocumented, talented youth in legal limbo. For those of us involved in this movement, there was no more waiting.

As the hunger strike began, many of us felt a sense of empowerment because we were taking ownership of our lives by engaging in direct action, despite the physical and political uncertainty.

Our fast took place on a busy intersection in Los Angeles, the corner of Santa Monica and Sepulveda Boulevards. For fifteen long days, twenty-four hours each day, we camped out in front of Senator Feinstein's office. The fast allowed me to reflect on the journeys undocumented immigrant youth embark on to survive in American society.

As an undocumented immigrant who, at the age of fourteen, came with my parents and siblings to the United States from Mexico, I have often faced discrimination and abuse from American citizens. My first job, at the age of seventeen, was as a night-shift janitor in a food service warehouse. I worked in this low-wage job, where I was paid under the table for several years, to pay for college. The warehouse workers treated me as if I were inferior, with no dignity or intelligence, speaking to me in slow and simple English, because they assumed I was not capable of understanding. They often told racist jokes in front of me, jokes riddled with derogatory stereotypes of immigrants and Mexicans. Many times the white employees carelessly dropped their trash on the floor in my presence, debasing my role in the workplace.

During the hunger strike, I interacted with the Senator's staff and came to understand how distant their politics were from our realities. I realized that the change we needed had to come from the people most affected by the broken US immigration system. Our voices and stories must become our tools to combat this oppressive system.

As the hunger strike progressed and the story of our struggle spread, we were joined by other undocumented youth and allies. Some joined our fast for several days in solidarity. We were visited by more than three hundred supporters from all walks of life. We shared our stories with pedestrians, news reporters, schoolchildren and mothers, and even police officers from the area who stopped by nightly to check on us. Every day that went by, our strike gained more notoriety. We grew stronger in our

At the culmination of our hunger strike, we held a candlelight vigil with sisters and brothers from all over Southern California, who came together outside Senator Feinstein's office to celebrate the end of our fifteen-day fast. Numerous community leaders, like Rabbi Jonathan Klein from Clergy and Laity United for Economic Justice in Los Angeles, joined us and spoke about the tradition of fasting for justice. Dreamers who participated in the hunger strike reflected on our experiences of fasting for our dream. Jorge Gutierrez, my friend and fellow dreamer who also fasted for the full fifteen days, was joined by his mother. He

As the hunger strike began, many of us felt a
sense of empowerment
because we were taking ownership of our lives
by engaging in **direct action**,
despite the physical and political uncertainty

identity as youth who were undocumented and unafraid, even as we saw the Department of Homeland Security vehicles drive by daily on their way to and from the Los Angeles Federal Building. Each night we crawled into our tents to sleep, with half the energy we'd had the night before. The cold winds from the ocean, only a few miles away, cut through our tents. We attempted to stay warm by using several layers of blankets, many donated by strangers who saw us on television or heard us on the radio.

The night shift, comprised of friends and supporters, held watch while we slept. On one of those nights, a loud bang woke us from our sleep. I was disoriented, but I heard reports from the night shift describing a gory car accident. Ambulances arrived on the scene a few minutes later. Our nights and days became longer, and while we knew that we faced safety hazards, ICE raids, and deteriorating health, our moral conviction for change grew stronger.

shared his story of coming out to her as a gay man and her unconditional love that has sustained him throughout his life. He discussed the challenges of being both undocumented and queer and how the hunger strike made him appreciate these intersecting identities. For him and other queer and undocumented dreamers who participated, the hunger strike was an affirmation of the importance of creating inclusive spaces in our movement that allow queer, undocumented dreamers to develop as leaders and heal as individuals.

The Los Angeles hunger strike was one action in our growing immigrant youth movement. Hunger strikes were also held in other parts of the country as part of the escalating campaign to demand that the DREAM Act be introduced as a stand-alone bill. Fifteen members of the New York Immigrant Youth Council fasted for ten days in June 2010 to pressure Senator Charles Schumer to champion the DREAM Act.

Three courageous undocumented women from the North Carolina Dream Team fasted for thirteen days seeking Senator Kay Hagan's vote and support. DREAM Act NOW held the largest and longest hunger strike, which began on November 10, 2010, at the University of Texas at San Antonio and lasted over forty-five days. Their target was Senator Kay Bailey Hutchison, who ended up not supporting the DREAM Act. In the weeks prior to the Senate vote on the DREAM Act in December 2010, hunger strikes were also held in Minnesota, Arizona, and Indiana.

The sacrifices that undocumented immigrant youth and allies made during our hunger strikes were not in vain. Though the ultimate goal of passing the DREAM Act fell short in the December 2010 Senate vote, thousands of people were moved by the stories of the hunger strikers, inspired by their actions, and mobilized to join this important cause.

I have lived as an undocumented immigrant in this country for twelve years. Since the hunger strike, I graduated with a master's degree in social work from UCLA as one of the first undocumented students to receive a UCLA graduate degree. I continue to reflect on what gives me strength to do the work that I do and to persevere against all odds. It disturbs me that some who support the DREAM Act argue that undocumented youth are not at fault for our situation, with the implication that it is our parents who are to blame. But for me, my parents have been my source of inspiration. My parents made the courageous decision and sacrifice to come to this country for a better future for my siblings and me. They have always stood with me to overcome every obstacle. During the hunger strike, my parents and sister spent a whole weekend by my side. They were the safety team at night and the cleaning crew in the morning. They looked out for me and provided moral support. My parents continue to do their best to help my sister and me to achieve our dreams. My participation in the hunger strike was not only an attempt to highlight the plight for undocumented immigrant youth striving for a dream but also a cry for dignity and humanity for all immigrant communities in this country.

Viridiana Martinez, Loida Silva, and Rosario Lopez on the first night of their hunger strike, June 13, 2010.
Courtesy of Justin Valas/NC DREAM Team.

the emergence of the immigrant youth movement

Matias Ramos and Cristina Jiménez

Today immigrant youth leaders are at the forefront of the immigrant rights movement. The leadership of young immigrants has strengthened the movement by injecting it with fresh energy, ideas, and innovative organizing strategies. Immigrant youth came together around the DREAM Act, first introduced in 2001, by recognizing our shared narrative. We were brought movement, but by 2008, immigrant youth were ready to lead and to push the DREAM Act to the center of the immigration debate.

United We Dream set out to develop a sustainable grassroots movement of immigrant youth and became a space where young people began to imagine what a movement for immigrant justice could look like. At first, it was only a slogan and a banner,

> by 2008, immigrant youth were
> **ready to lead and to push**
> the DREAM Act to the **center** of
> the immigration debate

to this country by our parents; we have grown up in this country and adopted American values and culture, but we are excluded from society because we lack legal immigration status.

In December 2008, United We Dream (UWD)—an informal coalition of immigrant youth, allies, and advocates—with support from the National Immigration Law Center, convened a national meeting of core leaders and immigrant youth organizations from across the country. At this meeting, immigrant youth leaders decided to take on the challenge of simultaneously building a national, immigrant-youth-led organization and leading the campaign to pass the DREAM Act, which had failed to pass the Senate in 2007. When the DREAM Act was first introduced, immigrant youth were led by advocates and lacked agency within the but eventually it became a nonprofit organization. In this network, immigrant youth are able to put ideas into action and transform the punitive labels that society places on us—"illegals" and "intruders"—into a source of limitless power: undocumented and unafraid.

Earlier that decade, many of us had shared the liberating experience of telling people close to us that we were undocumented and discovering that they were still loving and caring. Leaving the undocumented closet was about dreaming of something bigger, and so the movement grew. Through regional and national meetings and trainings, also known as Dream Camps, hundreds of undocumented students have been recruited, trained, and empowered to be full stakeholders in the work to change our current condition. This movement's power and growth was evident in the national congress convened by UWD in Memphis, Tennessee, in March 2010. More than two hundred immigrant youth leaders from fifty-five youth organizations representing twenty-two states came together to share their stories, sharpen their organizing skills, develop a national strategy to stop the deportations of DREAM-Act-eligible youth, and pass the DREAM Act. We came together again in November of 2011 for the largest gathering of its kind; over four hundred immigrant youth from thirty states met in Dallas, Texas, to celebrate our triumphs over the last decade of organizing, including the ten-year anniversary of in-state tuition for undocumented students in Texas.

Many of the early members of United We Dream went on to become activists creating the type of movement that builds on the pantheon of American student activism. Teams of young undocumented leaders from across the country spoke to senators face-to-face in the halls of Congress, walked into the public sphere courageously challenging a lifelong existence in the shadows, and willingly broke unjust laws to act on their most deeply held beliefs.

Eventually the United We Dream banner became too small to hold together a movement that was already vast and necessarily evolving. Other networks and initiatives added their voices to help create the multiplicity of actions necessary to build long-term societal change. Although UWD has focused on passing the DREAM Act, immigrant youth leaders are realizing that, as immigration enforcement and the persecution of immigrants intensifies, they must broaden their efforts. Fighting anti-immigration initiatives at the local level has become another target of their efforts, as in the case of Arizona's Senate Bill 1070 and similar proposals in Florida, Georgia, and Alabama. The organizing power of immigrant youth has become instrumental in fighting these local battles.

Immigrant youth's energy, commitment, courage, and leadership will continue to take the immigrant rights movement to the next level. This leadership role is empowering but also a great responsibility. Immigrant youth, however, are up to the challenge and ready to build power through an innovative and effective organizing infrastructure, along with a shared narrative of dreams, hopes, and a passion for justice.

November 2011. *Courtesy of Adrian Gonzalez.*

AFRICAN AMERICAN MINISTRIES IN ACTION (AAMIA), AMERICAN FEDERATION OF LABOR AND CONGRESS OF INDUSTRIAL ORGANIZATIONS (AFL-CIO), AMERICAN ASSOCIATION OF COMMUNITY COLLEGES, AMERICAN ASSOCIATION OF STATE COLLEGES AND UNIVERSITIES (AASCU), AMERICAN ASSOCIATION OF UNIVERSITY WOMEN (AAUW), AMERICAN COUNCIL ON EDUCATION, AMERICAN FEDERATION OF TEACHERS, AMERICAN HUMANE ASSOCIATION, AMERICAN JEWISH COMMITTEE, AMERICANS FOR DEMOCRATIC ACTION, INC., AMERICA'S VOICE, AMNESTY INTERNATIONAL USA, ANTI-DEFAMATION LEAGUE, ASIAN AMERICAN JUSTICE CENTER, ASIAN PACIFIC AMERICAN LABOR ALLIANCE, AFL-CIO, ASSOCIATION OF PUBLIC AND LAND-GRANT UNIVERSITIES (A-P-L-U), B'NAI B'RITH INTERNATIONAL, BOAT PEOPLE SOS, CATHOLIC LEGAL IMMIGRATION NETWORK, INC. (CLINIC), CENTER FOR LAW AND SOCIAL POLICY, CHILDREN'S DEFENSE FUND, CHRISTIANS FOR COMPREHENSIVE IMMIGRATION REFORM (CCIR), CHURCH WORLD SERVICE, COALITION ON HUMAN NEEDS, COUNCIL FOR OPPORTUNITY IN EDUCATION, DISCIPLES JUSTICE ACTION NETWORK, DISCIPLES OF CHRIST / EPISCOPAL CHURCH, EQUAL JUSTICE SOCIETY, FAMILY VIOLENCE PREVENTION FUND, FAMILY VOICES, INC., FIRST FOCUS CAMPAIGN FOR CHILDREN, FIRST STAR, FOSTER CARE ALUMNI OF AMERICA, HEBREW IMMIGRANT AID SOCIETY, HISPANIC ASSOCIATION OF COLLEGES AND UNIVERSITIES (HACU), HISPANIC FEDERATION, HUMAN RIGHTS FIRST, HMONG NATIONAL DEVELOPMENT, INC., INTERFAITH WORKER JUSTICE, IRISH APOSTOLATE USA, JAPANESE AMERICAN CITIZENS LEAGUE, JOINT CENTER FOR POLITICAL AND ECONOMIC STUDIES, LAB COUNCIL FOR LATIN AMERICAN ADVANCEMENT, LATINO JUSTICE PRLDEF, LAWYERS' COMMITTEE FOR CIVIL RIGHTS UNDER LAW, LEADERSHIP CONFERENCE ON CIVIL AND HUMAN RIGHTS (LCCR), LEGAL MOMENTUM, LUTHERAN IMMIGRANT AND REFUGEE SERVICE, MARIANIST SOCIAL JUSTICE COLLABORATIVE, MEXICAN AMERICAN LEGAL DEFENSE AND EDUCATIONAL FUND (MALDEF), MULTICULTURAL EDUCATION, TRAINING AND ADVOCACY (META), NAACP LEGAL DEFENSE AND EDUCATIONAL FUND, INC., NATIONAL ADVOCACY CENTER OF SISTERS OF THE GOOD SHEPHERD, NATIONAL ASSOCIATION FOR BILINGUAL EDUCATION (NABE), NATIONAL ASSOCIATION FOR COLLEGE ADMISSION COUNSELING, NATIONAL ASSOCIATION FOR THE EDUCATION AND ADVANCEMENT OF CAMBODIAN, LAOTIAN AND VIETNAMESE AMERICANS (NAFEA), NAFSA: ASSOCIATION FOR INTERNATIONAL EDUCATORS, NATIONAL ASSOCIATION FOR THE EDUCATION OF HOMELESS CHILDREN AND YOUTH, NATIONAL ASSOCIATION FOR MULTICULTURAL EDUCATION, NATIONAL ASSOCIATION OF WORKING WOMEN, NATIONAL ASSOCIATION OF SOCIAL WORKERS, NATIONAL COALITION FOR ASIAN PACIFIC AMERICAN COMMUNITY DEVELOPMENT, NATIONAL COUNCIL OF LA RAZA (NCLR), NATIONAL DAY LABORERS ORGANIZING NETWORK, NATIONAL DOMESTIC VIOLENCE HOTLINE, NATIONAL EDUCATION ASSOCIATION, NATIONAL EMPLOYMENT LAW PROJECT, NATIONAL FOSTER CARE COALITION, NATIONAL HISPANIC CHRISTIAN LEADERSHIP CONFERENCE, NATIONAL IMMIGRATION FORUM, NATIONAL IMMIGRATION LAW CENTER (NILC), NATIONAL KOREAN AMERICAN SERVICE AND EDUCATION CONSORTIUM (NAKASEC), NATIONAL LATINA INSTITUTE FOR REPRODUCTIVE HEALTH, NATIONAL PTA, NATIONAL WIC ASSOCIATION, NATIONAL WOMEN'S LAW CENTER, NATIONALITIES SERVICE CENTER, NETWORK, A NATIONAL CATHOLIC SOCIAL JUSTICE LOBBY, PEOPLE FOR THE AMERICAN WAY, PICO NATIONAL NETWORK, PROGRESSIVE JEWISH ALLIANCE, PUBLIC AFFAIRS ALLIANCE OF IRANIAN AMERICANS, PUBLIC EDUCATION NETWORK, SARGENT SHRIVER NATIONAL CENTER ON LAW AND POLICY, SCHOOL SOCIAL WORK ASSOCIATION OF AMERICA (SSWAA), SERVICE EMPLOYEES INTERNATIONAL UNION (SEIU), SOUTHEAST ASIA RESOURCE ACTION CENTER (SEARAC), TEACHERS OF ENGLISH TO SPEAKERS OF OTHER LANGUAGES (TESOL), THE COLLEGE BOARD, THE HISPANIC ASSOCIATION OF EVANGELICALS, THE NATIONAL ADVOCACY CENTER OF THE SISTERS OF GOOD SHEPHERD, THE UNITED CHURCH OF CHRIST, JUSTICE AND WITNESS MINISTRIES, UNION FOR REFORM JUDAISM, UNITARIAN UNIVERSALISTS ASSOCIATION OF CONGREGATIONS, UNITED CHURCH OF CHRIST, UNITED FOOD AND COMMERCIAL WORKERS INTERNATIONAL UNION (UFCW), UNITED METHODIST CHURCH, GENERAL BOARD OF CHURCH AND SOCIETY, UNITED STATES CONFERENCE OF CATHOLIC BISHOPS, UNITED STATES STUDENTS ASSOCIATION, UNITED WE DREAM NETWORK, VOICES FOR AMERICA'S CHILDREN, WESTERN ASSOCIATION OF COLLEGE ADMISSION COUNSELING, WIDER CHURCH MINISTRIES, WIDER OPPORTUNITIES FOR WOMEN, WIN - THE WELCOMING IMMIGRANTS NETWORK, YOUNG PEOPLE FOR ACTION, YWCA USA

I Support the DREAM ACT

Iconic buttons distributed by Dreamactivist.org and originally designed by activist Mario.

dream summer
David Cho, Nancy Meza, and Kent Wong

The UCLA Labor Center and the United We Dream Network launched a national internship program for DREAM Act student leaders in the summer of 2011 called Dream Summer. This ten-week internship placed over a hundred DREAM Act student leaders with social-justice, labor, and community organizations in California, Arizona, Florida, Washington, DC, and New York. An important part of the program involved assisting participants in identifying and applying for scholarship funds to help complete their education. Most importantly, Dream Summer was a program run by and for immigrant youth to deliver unprecedented leadership development and internship opportunities.

Rev. James Lawson Jr. speaks to Dream Summer interns.
Courtesy of Pocho1.

Dream Summer provided talented and capable immigrant youth activists with internship placements in social-justice organizations throughout the country, while strengthening the commitment of these organizations to advance the rights of immigrant youth. Dream Summer also financed urgently needed scholarships for immigrant students to pursue their educational goals and supported the expansion of a national network of activists on campus.

The Dream Summer internship began with a three-day retreat in June and concluded with a three-day retreat in September, both hosted by the UCLA Downtown Labor Center. The energy in the room during the retreats was powerful. Dream Summer interns honed their organizing skills, discussed campaign strategies, and developed personal narratives. Together, they laughed, cried, and built solidarity.

Veteran civil rights activist Rev. James Lawson Jr. opened the first retreat by sharing lessons from the Civil Rights Movement and drawing parallels between it and today's undocumented student movement: "For DREAM Act students, going to college is itself an act of civil disobedience." MALDEF (Mexican American Legal Defense and Educational Fund) President Tom Saenz and California Assemblymember Gilbert Cedillo, the champion of the California Dream Act, also spoke before the Dream Summer interns, expressing admiration and support for their determination and courage.

The first retreat concluded with an opening reception for an art show at the UCLA Downtown Labor Center celebrating the beautiful art, posters, and photography of the DREAM Act movement. Hundreds of dreamers and supporters gathered to enjoy the art, listen to live music and spoken word, watch short video documentaries of the movement, hear speeches, and dance.

At the closing retreat, Dream Summer participants shared their internship experiences and planned future work together, including Dream Summer 2012. On September 5, Dream Summer participants joined the Los Angeles Labor Day march, chanting "Undocumented and Unafraid!"

In their brief ten-week internships, Dream Summer interns worked to successfully pass California Assembly Bill 130 and the California Dream Act and organized support for the companion Assembly Bill 131. Interns contributed to the first US Senate hearing on the federal DREAM Act, educated the community on the change in policy implemented to curtail the deportation of DREAM-Act-eligible students, and participated in the first undocumented student civil disobedience arrest in California, held in San Bernardino. Dream Summer interns spoke before twenty-five hundred college financial aid officers; addressed fifteen hundred people at a rally in Oakland, California, as part of the national Asian Pacific American Labor Alliance convention; spoke out through local and national TV, radio, newspapers, and magazines; and organized educational conferences, town hall meetings, and press conferences throughout the country. The interns also organized car wash workers in Los Angeles, airport workers in Florida, and janitors in New York.

The Dream Summer interns' experiences were documented through film, photographs, and journals. The bonds developed among the interns continue to grow along with the immigrant youth movement. Preparations are already underway to organize future Dream Summers to include more cities, more states, and more DREAM Act leaders.

Dream Summer provided talented and **capable immigrant youth** activists with internship placements in social-justice organizations **throughout the country**

Dream Summer 2011 interns march in the Labor Day parade in San Pedro, California. *Courtesy of Pocho1.*

undocumented youth chart new spaces for resistance:
blogging, tweeting, facebooking, and g-chatting the revolution

Prerna Lal and Flavia de la Fuente

One of the most dynamic elements of the immigrant youth movement has been our ability to drive our own actions and campaigns, fueled by the power of social media. Of course this does not replace door-to-door advocacy; rather, it is a readily accessible tool used to augment our efforts.

In late 2007, seven undocumented students came together in a virtual chat room on a DREAM Act forum to talk about the need for an action-oriented site. We purchased campaigns. It didn't take money—it just took attitude and initiative.

Dreamactivist.org welcomes over two thousand unique visitors per day and peaked at over seven thousand visitors per day during prime DREAM Act campaign season. There are a hundred thousand members on our e-mail list. This number continues to rise as we grow our movement offline. Our site is completely run by volunteers who are driven by their dedication

With virtually no organizing or social media skills, **we taught ourselves** how to use the technology and resources available to **build a new powerhouse** in the world of immigrant rights

a domain called Dreamactivist.org for ten dollars. With little infrastructure, twenty-somethings who had never met in person were sitting at our computers, blogging our mission and our message. Connecting our web site to various social networking platforms created a web of interaction accessible from multiple points at relatively little cost. With virtually no organizing or social media skills, we taught ourselves how to use the technology and resources available to build a new powerhouse in the world of immigrant rights, with a following that rivaled that of multimillion dollar public relations

to the immigrant youth movement. We also give visitors the opportunity to comment and contribute to our efforts. We have found that this online revolution funds itself.

There is certainly power in organized "clicks." A notable example is how immigrant youth activists use what is available online to centralize specific campaigns, such as stopping or deferring the deportation of a particular student. At first, without help or support from the existing nonprofit world, immigrant youth excelled where immigration lawyers failed. We built parallel structures of support to battle final removal orders issued against DREAM-Act-eligible students. We also shed light on the criminalization and detention of young immigrants. By combining online e-mail blasts with community support and phone calls directed to the right decision makers, immigrant youth successfully stopped dozens of deportations. These activities created a model that has since been replicated by many organizations and for many different communities.

Dozens of other undocumented youth have taken to social media to share our unique struggles, using microblogs such as Twitter and Tumblr as a way to facilitate critical discussions and organize civil disobedience actions in the real world. We use Facebook to update our social circles about public activities, and late-night G-Chat conversations lead to brainstorming sessions on our next steps. We have built borderless spheres of resistance that continue to grow as we adapt to new communications technology.

Ultimately what undocumented students have done online is build a community of activists across the country who identify with one another. We discuss our issues in a holistic, direct way, with no shame or fear—conversations we hope lead to much needed dialogue in our communities. In this world, undocumented youth may have never met one another, but we share a trust and bond that is grounded in recognition that we are in similar circumstances and united for a common purpose. More than strategy or money, this bond is what fuels the network.

Immigrant youth across the country organized a week of call-in actions to Congress in support of the Dream Act when it was introduced during the lame-duck session in 2010.
Design by Freddy Pech.

the fight to stop my deportation

Matias Ramos

The last ten years have been a time of unprecedented immigrant youth activism, and I have been proud to be a part of it. My family came to the United State from Argentina in 1999. My father, an accounts manager, lost his job during the Argentine economic crisis triggered in part by the policies advanced by global corporations. He decided his best hope to survive was to come to the United States to find work as an accountant. We were economic migrants in a world of migrating capital.

My mother, a kindergarten teacher by training, underwent the career transition many immigrants do when coming to America. She worked in the food service industry at Jack in the Box, the manufacturing industry in a sweatshop-like packaging company, and the immigrant entrepreneur industry, selling empanadas to fellow churchgoers. At the same time, my parents raised their children and held on to the same American dream they embraced

when they entered the country: the belief that hard work and a commitment to education would result in a better life for us.

I learned English as a teenager reading *Catcher in the Rye*, watching World Wrestling Entertainment, and enjoying Top 40 hits. I did well in school and attended UCLA, where I was one of the leaders of IDEAS. One of my transformative events while at UCLA was a road trip with Tam and Cinthya to Seattle to get our driver's licenses. Because California prohibits undocumented immigrants from obtaining licenses, we traveled to the state of Washington, where policies were more relaxed. Road trips are a rite of passage for many young people, but ours had a much more significant purpose. We were able to get licenses that could establish our identities, prove our dates of birth, allow us to travel, and afford privileges that most students take for granted.

At UCLA I worked on a campus radio

Undocumented youth protest outside an immigrant detention center in Texas. *Courtesy of Adrian Gonzalez.*

show, wrote extensively about immigrant youth issues, and contributed to the publication *Underground Undergrads: UCLA Undocumented Immigrant Students Speak Out*, which captured my story and that of other undocumented classmates. College was a time when I carefully reflected on my condition as an undocumented person. Even though I was an adult, I was less than a second-class citizen, with no path to legalize my status. And to the government, I was a criminal, though I had broken no law.

The last decade of undocumented youth activism has been marked by a dramatic intensification of immigration enforcement. Increased budgets for border patrols, criminalization of immigrants, and biometrics-based identification systems are part of a large-scale government crackdown

undocumented immigrant students and allies working for social change.

But the risks caught up with me. In February 2010, after attending a United We Dream meeting in Minnesota, I was detained at the Minneapolis airport by an overzealous Transportation Security Administration agent and turned over to the border patrol. Two days later, I was given an order of deportation. Fellow Dream Act students, supporters, and immigrant rights advocates launched a national campaign to stop my deportation. My deportation order was temporarily suspended, I was instructed to renew my Argentine passport, and I was granted temporary work authorization. Since then, my life has been in limbo. Immigration purgatory has become my reality.

More than **one million people** have been deported over the last three years, giving the Obama administration the dubious distinction of deporting **more people in one term** than the George W. Bush administration did in two

on undocumented immigrants. Deportations are on the rise, and the fear in immigrant communities is escalating.

Despite these increased risks, I took a chance to travel around the country to see what changes could be made and what people were doing to fight the backlash against immigrants. After graduating, I worked as an intern at the UCLA Labor Center and went on speaking tours to educate student, labor, and community organizations about the plight of immigrant youth. I went public with my story and appeared on national television, on the radio, and in newspapers. In April 2009, I moved to Washington, DC, to volunteer full time to work for the passage of the federal DREAM Act. I was one of the founding board members of United We Dream, the national network of

Tam was especially helpful during this time. She was used to routine check-ins with ICE. Although she could not be deported because of her "stateless" status, she still had to report regularly to the closest ICE office. She said, "Go at the end of the day. If you go early, they are going to make you wait for hours. But if you catch them at the end of the day, they are rushing to go home. They have families to go home to." Tam and I chatted after my first report date with ICE, but a few months later, she and Cinthya were gone, and I still miss them deeply.

A year and a half later, my immigration case took a turn for the worse. In September 2011, when I reported to the ICE office in Virginia for a routine check-in, without warning or notice, I was placed under a strict supervision program. They confiscated my passport and placed a thick rubber and plastic shackle on my ankle. For ten miserable days, I was forced to wear an electronic GPS monitoring device twenty-four hours a day. Every few hours, it would bark out strange commands until I pressed a button to make it stop. Some instructions were clear: "Call your officer," or "Recharge the battery." But on other occasions, the voice on the speaker ominously warned, "Leaving your master inclusion zone." I had to stand by a wall socket three hours each day to recharge the battery.

The shackling device is one of the dehumanizing tools used by a private company with a lucrative contract with the Department of Homeland Securities, paid for by US taxpayers. To the private contractor monitoring my every move, I was one more undocumented immigrant being subjected to degrading treatment for profit.

As an immigrant rights activist living in our nation's capital, I was no stranger to the massive and inhumane deportation system that has defined US immigration policy in the twenty-first century. More than one million people have been deported over the last three years, giving the Obama administration the dubious distinction of deporting more people in one term than the George W. Bush administration did in two.

As a result of a national campaign, the shackle was removed from my ankle. But for many months, dozens of DREAM-Act-eligible students have been similarly detained, shackled, and threatened with deportation. Each case that comes to the public light has mobilized thousands of people to stop the deportation. And we have succeeded in stopping dozens of deportations of immigrant youth.

But each case to deport dreamers is a huge waste of government resources and represents an immoral policy that victimizes young people who want nothing more than to contribute to this country. The failure of Congress to pass the DREAM Act and comprehensive immigration reform is harming immigrant youth, immigrant communities, and our society as a whole.

I am part of a growing movement demanding that the Obama administration use administrative relief to stop the deportation of DREAM-Act-eligible students and grant us work authorization. This would be in the best interests of my fellow dreamers, our families, and our communities, and would allow us to use our skills and talents to give back to this country we call home.

Despite the setbacks and constant uncertainty, I feel hopeful. The Dream movement is winning, and our campaign to secure the humane treatment of immigrant youth will one day be fulfilled.

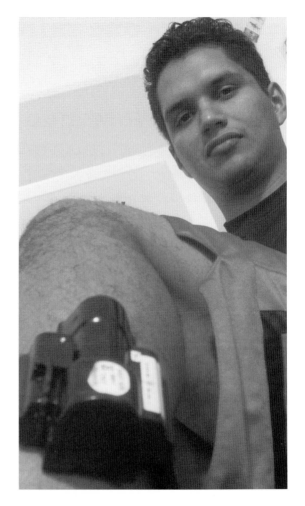

Courtesy of Matias Ramos.

breaking down closet doors:
queer and undocumented

Jorge Gutierrez, Imelda Plascencia,
and the Queer Undocumented Youth Collective

We are people and with the people we stand,
breaking borders and stereotypes,
like this system exploiting our hands.
—Yosimar Reyes,
"For Colored Boys Who Speak Softly"

"Coming out of the closet" is a phrase
that expresses the difficult yet rewarding
process of self-discovery and declaration
of our queer identity. But for queer undocumented youth, there are two closets that
we must break out of: our legal status and
our sexual orientation or gender identity.
We are taught to stay silent about these
realities because our identities are different
and unfamiliar. Both attributes invoke fear
in our society and sadly, we learn to feel
shame. Despite being conditioned to hide
in these closets, we choose to speak: we are
queer and undocumented, never one without the other.

These intersecting identities have
molded our contributions to the immigrant
youth movement. They designate who we
are when we walk through the door for a
meeting, as we wear our caps and gowns
to join a DREAM Act rally, and when we
get arrested in a civil disobedience action.
It is necessary to acknowledge and affirm
our identities and create a safe space for us
to express them. We face hatred and ignorance not just from those who discriminate
against queer individuals but also from
those who attack immigrants. Our experience is frequently ignored, misrepresented,
or ridiculed by a dominant culture.

We exist and organize at the marginalized intersections of our identities. At times

the use of homophobic language within
mainstream immigrant rights circles and
the lack of knowledge and compassion
about immigrant issues in queer spaces
make us feel that only part of ourselves
can be acknowledged at once. We lesbian/
gay/bisexual/transgender/queer dreamers
and allies are responsible for intention-
ally creating safe spaces for those who still
feel they have to negotiate for their place in
the movement.

"Queer, Undocumented, and Unafraid."
Illustration by Julio Salgado.

But for queer undocumented youth,
there are two closets that we must break out of—
our legal status and our
sexual orientation or gender identity

Although queer activists have been an integral part of many movements, often this history is untold. Queer black activist Bayard Rustin was a key civil rights leader in the 1960s and one of Martin Luther King Jr.'s close allies. Rustin was the chief organizer of the historic 1963 March on Washington and led the A. Philip Randolph Institute to promote black union leadership. Yet his contribution is often left out of history books, and he was discouraged from being public about his sexual orientation.

In the DREAM Act movement, queer student Felipe Matos was one of the leaders of the Trail of Dreams in 2010. While on their arduous, and at times physically dangerous, fifteen-hundred-mile mile journey on foot, Felipe and his partner were persuaded by some immigrant rights advocates to not talk about their relationship, express affection toward each other, or even hint at their sexual orientation. For five months, they walked hundreds of miles alongside one another from Miami to Washington, DC. Together they faced the Ku Klux Klan and other racist groups but were advised to keep their queer identities in the closet. Felipe's story is a clear example of the painful negotiations queer undocumented youth confront throughout the nation. It is essential that our stories continue to be shared in order for our needs to be addressed, our lives acknowledged, and our perspectives validated. Three of our stories follow.

Tony Choi

I still can't make sense of what was going through my mind that night. Jorge Gutierrez was presenting a workshop on queer undocumented youth at the United We Dream retreat in Memphis, Tennessee, and asked the audience to share their identities if they felt comfortable. I originally planned to talk with him after the session to thank him for speaking out. But one by one, I saw dreamers walk toward the stage, and something in my heart began to stir. That's when I decided to announce publicly, for the first time, that I am queer and unashamed. With a bizarre force, I threw down my jacket and walked toward the stage. Others who were there that night say that I ran to the stage. While the microphone was being passed around, I was paralyzed with fear. By the time it reached me, I felt as if a dam had broken in my heart. Everything I had been holding within me began to release as tears welled up in my eyes. All of the stories I kept inside me started flooding my thoughts.

"동성애자가 되지마!" "No seas maricon!" "Don't be a fag!" All of the heartbreaks that I endured in solitude, all of the bullying that I lived through in middle school and high school, and everything else that I kept silent inside of me surfaced, and I broke through my isolation that night. I was able to share a part of me with two hundred people, and a sudden realization came to me that I didn't have to be alone anymore. After all, those who came before me were there with me, and I was leading the way for others to come. I was standing on the shoulders of giants.

I still don't know how I'm going to face the future. I admit it, I'm still afraid of what will be there after tomorrow. I have an endless stream of questions in my head about how to approach this. How will I talk to my friends? What about my family? Should I have a coming-out party with rainbow decor? Should I silently click on "Men" in the "Interested In" check box on Facebook? I'm still trying to figure everything out. But now the fight is different. I'm not alone in this, and I'm certainly not ashamed of who I am, because this is how God wonderfully created me. Let me introduce myself to you: My name is Tony, I am undocumented, queer, unashamed, and I'm learning to be unafraid.

Grecia Mondragon

I live with the everyday struggle and challenge that comes with being a part of more than one marginalized community. I'm an undocumented and queer *mujer* raised in a conservative family. I'm the first of five children to attend college and the eldest daughter. All of this comes with expectations and responsibilities. I'm required to fulfill certain gender roles within my culture and family, rules thought by some to be broken because I am queer. Within my Latino Christian family, it is expected that I will form a family and create a home with a man. I do desire to form a family with children but with the understanding that a family is not just formed between a man and a woman. The definition of a family should not be predetermined by society but rather by individuals who love each other.

I'm not different; I just want to be happy and respected for who I am. My rights as a human being are limited because I am undocumented, and my civil liberties are violated simply because I am trying to be myself. I'm frustrated with having to wait for legislation to pass in order to grant me the right to live in a country that is already my home, and I am tired of the rhetoric that insinuates I need permission to be queer. I want to be treated equally, and so I turn to God, because it is my faith that gives me hope every day.

The Queer Undocumented Youth Collective leads a discussion. *Courtesy of Pocho1.*

Tony Ortuno

I came out to my mom as a gay man at the age of twenty. It was a warm night in July. We sat on her bed and when the words came out of me, "Soy Gay," "I'm Gay," I saw tears flow down her cheeks. She attempted to decipher what went "wrong" in my life to lead me to this point. A year has passed, and it seems like we have this conversation time and time again. She has yet to recognize and accept who I am. Despite our conflicts about my queer identity, we are very much connected through the identity we do share: our undocumented status.

I am empowered by my intersecting realities because they are a part of me, but they invoke fear in my mother. I hope that one day she can see me for who I still am: her son. Until then, I wait for the day when she joins me in the fight for our rights. One day, she and I will be unafraid, together.

asian american, undocumented, and unafraid

Catherine Eusebio

My family moved from the Philippines to a suburb in the San Francisco Bay Area when I was four years old. Although I have some hazy memories of living in the Philippines, I did not see myself as an immigrant. After all, I came to America already fluent in English and expected any vestige of my foreign past to disappear along with my accent. By the time I began school, I thought I was an American just like everyone else. I made friends easily with other students and fit in with Filipino American-born girls. Like me, they knew all the lyrics to Backstreet Boys and Spice Girls songs. We all looked

ASPIRE members worked to elect the first undocumented student senator, Ju Hong, at UC Berkeley, 2010. *Courtesy of ASPIRE.*

forward to Friday nights to watch *Boy Meets World* and *Sabrina, the Teenage Witch*. We all shopped at Old Navy, sporting different colored versions of the same outfits.

Eventually, however, I began to discover that my friends and I were not really the same. As I became more aware of my immigration status, I felt tremendous social pressure to lie. I had to cover up these differences to live up to the Asian American middle-class norm. In doing so, I perpetuated the "model minority" myth, the belief that all Asian Americans are successful or could easily overcome any barriers to success.

In elementary school, I was disrespectful to my mother so that I could relate to other children. When a classmate asked about my family's apartment, "There are at least two bedrooms, right?" I lied by nodding in tacit agreement. Unlike my friends who had their own rooms in large houses, my family lived in a one-bedroom apartment. Even though I didn't know about green cards and social security numbers at the time, I began to see the connections; our station in life was tied to being a newly arrived immigrant family.

In high school, I lied to distance myself from my father. When asked what he did for a living, I replied unconvincingly, "I don't know." It was half true. I didn't know what my dad did day to day. But I knew that like other "illegals," my father worked under the table in construction. I didn't want to be associated with a vilified stereotype. While my friends' fathers dressed for their nine-to-five jobs in dark blue business suits, my dad came home with paint splattered jeans and dirty boots, when he was lucky enough to secure a job.

I also deceived myself, placing my absolute faith in the American dream. Despite recognizing these differences about my family, I believed that it just didn't matter where I came from, who my parents were, or how much money my family made. It just mattered that I worked hard. If I worked hard, I could pull myself up by the bootstraps and live up to the model minority myth of success.

After I had been accepted to several campuses in the University of California system, my mom finally made me accept the

community-based organization Asian Law Caucus (ALC). In seeking their own path to legalization, three undocumented young clients of ALC discovered that their only solution was to advocate for comprehensive changes in immigration laws. ASPIRE evolved from a support network into an advocacy organization.

ASPIRE strategizes and organizes for the passage of immigrant-friendly legislation at the federal and state levels. Our members have pushed local college presidents and chancellors to release public letters of support for the federal DREAM Act. In fall 2010 during a crucial period for

Having a space for undocumented
Asians to gather together allows us to
take the first step in recognizing that
we need each other

truth. With hot tears flowing down my face, I asked, "Mom, why can't I go to my university?" She replied, "You don't have papers. Even if you bled me dry, we still wouldn't have enough money for your school." No matter how hard I tried, I just couldn't have the same experiences and privileges as my American-born friends. While my friends were scattering all over California to go to prestigious universities, I was anchored in my hometown to—in my mind—a lowly community college. I blamed my parents for making me feel powerless and isolated.

My anger and resentment toward my parents slowly gave way to the desire to create social change. I didn't want to live as a victim in an unjust world. I wanted to do something about my status. My entry into the immigrant youth movement came through Asian Students Promoting Immigrant Rights through Education (ASPIRE) in San Francisco. The first Asian undocumented student group in the nation, ASPIRE was created in 2008 through the

the campaign, we organized daily phone-banking sessions for community members to call US senators to urge them to vote for the bill. At the state level, we lobbied legislators in Sacramento to vote for the California Dream Act, a financial aid bill that helps undocumented youth in California fund their college dreams. APIRE has recently joined with coalitions in the state of California, such as the California Dream Team Alliance, where we strategize and collaborate on different campaigns that advance the rights of immigrants in California. Our members have also branched out and participated in civil disobedience actions in partnership with a range of other organizations. Through our work, ASPIRE has become a respected partner in the immigrant youth movement.

Most importantly, ASPIRE has worked to transform attitudes within the Asian American community. Our culture encourages us to silence the stories that deviate from societal expectations. But in doing so, we miss the opportunity to create change. ASPIRE directly challenges this expectation not only by being visible and taking action but also by creating the space for dialogue within our community. ASPIRE spearheaded the first Asian immigrant youth conference at the University of California, Berkeley, to explore the issues that we have not had the opportunity to discuss collectively. Some of these issues include mental health, undocumented women and violence, and the intersecting identities of queer students in the Asian undocumented student movement.

The culture of shame and silence is changing. In the past year, students have come to us from all over California to help establish their own undocumented Asian student groups. There is now a strong ASPIRE group at UCLA working in conjunction with IDEAS at UCLA to create a support and advocacy group for undocumented students on campus.

ASPIRE has also helped me personally transform. I have finally begun to heal. I no longer blame my parents. Learning about the flawed immigration system and the politics that have prevented reform has allowed me to recognize what my parents have done for me and what blessings they have shared with me. My mother sacrificed all that she had in the Philippines so that I could have a better life. Despite the meager earnings from hours of physical toil, my father always made sure to give me an allowance so that I could save money toward my education. My father worked as a day laborer, so that I wouldn't have to one day.

Having a space for undocumented Asians to gather together allows us to take the first step in recognizing that we need each other. Had I continued to ignore my status by trying to fit in, I would not have been moved to fight for social injustice. ASPIRE has helped to create the space we need to empower ourselves.

ASPIRE conference, October 2011. *Courtesy of ASPIRE.*

different experiences, similar fears:
asian pacific islander and latina/o undocumented student experiences

Abigail Bangalon, Margarita Peralta, and Laura E. Enriquez

"Undocumented" is very racialized. Latino or Latina is a synonym for undocumented.
—Christina Guzman, interviewee

When they think of undocumented, they mostly think of Hispanics or Mexicans. They don't see the Asian community or other ethnic groups.
—Miriam Delgado, interviewee

Pilipinos are considered Asians, and people have the image that all Asians are smart.
—Jennifer O'Campo, interviewee

Just being Latino makes people second guess your legality . . . .
—Ricky Gomez, interviewee

Throughout US history, Asian Pacific Islander (API) and Latina/o populations have been stereotyped, both positively and negatively. While any foreigner could potentially be undocumented, current anti-immigrant rhetoric focuses primarily on the Latina/o population. Because mainstream media and academic research on undocumented students also emphasize Latina/o experiences, issues surrounding the undocumented API community experience have been generally unexplored (Buenavista et al 2010).

Popular discourse surrounding this subject stereotypes Latina/os negatively as illegal aliens, while the API stereotype is one of a model minority, a seemingly positive stereotype that regards the API pathway to success as a model for other minority groups to follow (Chavez 2008, 23;

Chen 1991, 167). Examples of this stereotype depict API students as math geniuses, computer science experts, and high-school valedictorians. In contrast, the general portrayals of Latina/o students are negative, emphasizing their educational and economic failures, in contrast to the successes of their API counterparts. Thus, it is not surprising that a common misconception in the United States is that undocumented students are solely Latina/o, when in fact, roughly half of the undocumented students in the University of California system emigrate from Asia and the Pacific Islands (Kim 2010; UCOP Student Financial Support 2010).

Studies and reports that look at the DREAM Act also tend to emphasize the Latina/o population. For example, Gonzalez's 2009 College Board Advocacy report states that "there were 11.9 million undocumented migrants living in the United States. They represent countries from around the globe, but most come from Latin America: Of the 9.6 million unauthorized immigrants from Latin American countries, 7 million are from Mexico." Similarly, Batalova and Fix (2006) and Valenzuela and Escudero (2009) do not disaggregate data by racial and ethnic categories. Even though an overwhelming majority of undocumented students are indeed Latina/o, studies like these can obscure the fact that undocumented students are diverse and hail from different parts of the globe. Our research shows that 12.3 percent of the DREAM-Act-eligible population is Asian or Pacific Islander.

Since the racial heterogeneity of the undocumented population is often ignored, we seek to fill this gap by examining racial stereotypes and how they affect each ethnic group's identity, status, and access to resources. In addition, we explore the common struggles and fears that API and Latina/o undocumented students share throughout their life journeys. We first present a brief demographic profile of undocumented youth. We then analyze our interviews with undocumented youth with a particular focus on the impact of stereotypes on API and Latina/o students. To protect their confidentiality, participants' names have been changed and personal information has been obscured. "Latina/o" is defined as a person who is Puerto Rican, Mexican, Cuban, or Central or South American, and who self-identifies as a member of the Latina/o ethnic group (Gonzales 2002). "Asian" refers to those having origins in any of the original peoples of the Far East,

Southeast Asia, or the Indian subcontinent, including, for example, Cambodia, China, India, Japan, Korea, Malaysia, Pakistan, the Philippine Islands, Thailand, and Vietnam. "Pacific Islander" refers to those having origins in any of the original peoples of Hawaii, Guam, Samoa, or other Pacific Islands (Reeves 2003).

Racialized Experiences and Access to Resources: Comparing the Experiences of Undocumented Latina/os and Asian Pacific Islanders

Latina/os are often blamed for the country's immigration problems and stigmatized as illegal aliens. This generalization occurs not only in popular conversations and the media but also in certain academic publications (Chavez 2008; Perez 2009). While the continuous portrayal of Latina/os as undocumented perpetuates a negative stereotype, it has also opened a space for resource allocation and some benefits (Chan 2009). While API undocumented youth do not experience the same negative stereotyping as Latina/os do, their invisibility has led to less community support and limited access to information and resources.

Undocumented Racialization: Hiding Your Status

Latina/o undocumented students have more difficulty passing as legal residents than their API peers. Esperanza Vargas is an undocumented student from Mexico. Although Esperanza does not have an accent, she believes her Latina heritage encourages the assumption that she is undocumented: "People don't realize there are a lot of undocumented immigrants from Asia. When you think undocumented, you think of Mexico and Latin America. I think it would be easier to pass as documented if I were another race." Many of the students we spoke to made similar comments that demonstrate the connections between their notions of race, racial stereotypes, and undocumented status.

Courtesy of Adrian Gonzalez.

API undocumented [youth] **invisibility** has led to less community support and **limited access** to information and resources

Pablo Ortiz explains that these stereotypes have important consequences: "It's hard for me being dark-skinned. My English pronunciation is not great. It's just luggage that I carry on my back that they're going to recognize my accent, point me out, and say, 'You're undocumented.' My skin color [also makes people assume] that I'm undocumented." Latina/o heritage coupled with dark skin tone and an accent, can increase the perception that one is undocumented. Light-skinned Latina/os and APIs are less likely to be suspected of being undocumented.

Mary Magpayo, a Filipina undocumented student, explains how people regularly assume she is a citizen. Mary retells a recent experience when she was approached by a volunteer to fill out a voter registration form. She said no, but the volunteer persisted until Mary told him that she was not a citizen. The volunteer then responded, "Well, you look like a citizen." This left Mary puzzled over how she can be seen as a citizen but not be one at the same time. She believes her Filipina heritage allows her to avoid being identified as undocumented.

Instead of dealing with the illegal immigrant stigma, APIs deal with the model minority stereotype, a common misconception that APIs achieve a higher level of academic success than the average population. As a member of the model minority, one is expected to assimilate, perform well in school, and obey the rules (Lee 1996). Zeus Yun explains, "Others assume Asians are strict people who always follow the law. How can they be undocumented?" Amanda Su reflects on being Korean and undocumented: "Knowing how many stereotypes are out there, I would say that there would be more stereotypes against me if I would have been of a different ethnic background . . . ." Amanda believes API undocumented students can navigate educational institutions more easily, because their legal status is not constantly called into question.

Accessing Resources

While Latina/os face more negative stereotypes, they also may have greater access to resources and social support because of the large Latina/o youth population and the existence of organizations advocating for undocumented immigrants. The experience of joining an undocumented student organization is easier for Latina/os, as many campuses have established organizations that reach out to incoming students within the Latina/o community. However, there is limited information available to undocumented API students. Even basic materials on how to apply for college are only in Spanish or English (Chan 2008). This is a significant barrier to APIs who speak limited English and who need to access resources in their native language or within their communities.

Sylvia Muñoz is a member of her university's undocumented student organization. She describes her first experience attending a meeting and the instant connection she felt: "They were welcoming. I was seen as another family member and it's becoming my other house, where I can rely on people. I know a lot of people who are there, and they support you." On the other hand, Zeus, an undocumented Mongolian student, feels like an outsider because there are only two or three undocumented APIs in his organization: "In a way, it made me feel lonely. I didn't have anyone else to speak to about Mongolia. I didn't have anybody to speak to in my own language."

Shared Experiences

Undocumented APIs and Latina/os experience similar problems related to their lack of legal authorization. Both groups struggle to conceal their immigration status for fear of being judged by peers or others in their networks. Disclosing their status may lead to disapproval, making them feel different or isolated.

The Filipino community uses the popular derogatory expression, *tago ng tago*, which literally means "always hiding" (Chan 2009). This expression refers to undocumented immigrants who hide and move from place to place to avoid deportation. Mary reflects on being Filipino and undocumented: "When you are Filipino, your family tends to hide you in the shadows. They don't want to reveal your identity [as] undocumented because there is a shame that comes with it. It impact[s] their image as well."

Similarly, Adrian Perez talks about his experience with having to conceal his status: "In my junior year [of high school], everyone was sending [in college] applications. My counselor wanted me to apply to Berkeley. She just assumed I would get a full ride because of my grades and my mom's income. But when I told her that I did not have papers, she did not know what to do. It made me feel different . . . it made me feel as if I was doing something wrong. After that I became very cautious as to whom I would trust with that type of information. So I went throughout my school without ever telling anybody except one friend, but

"Not Just a Latino Issue." *Illustration by Julio Salgado.*

he did not like it. That made me fear trusting someone with that information." As a result of the negative reaction from his friend, Adrian chose to keep silent: "Very few of my friends actually know. It's something I usually don't talk about unless the situation presents itself where I need to tell them. I don't want to feel any different."

Like Adrian and Mary, many undocumented immigrant students keep their status a secret. It is a secret they must conceal every day. As undocumented students, they are denied access to work opportunities, to education, and to financial aid. They contend with the possibility of rejection by people they trust, including close friends and mentors. In this sense, undocumented Latina/o and API students face the same fears and struggles.

References

Batalova, Jeanne, and Michael Fix. 2006. "New Estimates of Unauthorized Youth Eligible for Legal Status under the DREAM Act." Migration Policy Institute, *Immigration Backgrounder* 1 (October). http://www.migrationpolicy.org/pubs/Backgrounder1_Dream_Act.pdf.

Buenavista, Tracy Lachica, Angela Chua-Ru, and Tam Tran. 2010. "Undocumented Asian American Experiences: Highlighting the Parallels between 'Model Minority' and Undocumented Student Discourses." Unpublished manuscript, last modified November 10, 2010. Microsoft Word file.

Chan, Beleza. 2008. "Not 'a Mexican Thing': Undocumented Asian Students Face Stigma and Lack of Financial Aid, Job Experience," *Asian Week*, October 13. http://www.asianweek.com/2008/10/13/not-mexican-thing-undocumented-asian-students-face-stigma-and-lack-of-financial-aid-job-experience/.

Chan, Beleza. 2009. "Not Just a Latino Issue: Undocumented Students in Higher Education," *Journal of College Admission* 206: 29–31. http://www.e4fc.org/images/CHAN_NACAC_NOTJUSTLATINO.pdf.

Chen, Sucheng. 1991. *Asian Americans: An Interpretive History.* Immigrant Heritage of America Series. New York: Twayne Publishers.

Chavez, Leo R. 2008. *The Latino Threat: Constructing Immigrants, Citizens, and the Nation.* Stanford: Stanford University Press.

Gonzalez, Roberto G. 2009. "Young Lives on Hold: The College Dreams of Undocumented Students." *College Board Advocacy.* http://advocacy.collegeboard.org/sites/default/files/young-lives-on-hold-summary-cb.pdf.

Gonzales, Patricia, Hart Blanton, and Kevin J. Williams. 2002. "The Effects of Stereotype Threat and Double-Minority Status on the Test Performance of Latino Women." *Personality and Social Psychology Bulletin* 28, (5): 659–670. doi: 10.1177/0146167202288010.

Kim, Minsuk. 2010. "Korean Americans March for America." *The Huffington Post.* March 17. http://www.huffingtonpost.com/minsuk-kim/korean-americans-march-fo_b_503329.html.

Lee, Stacey J. 1996. *Unraveling the "Model Minority" Stereotype: Listening to Asian American Youth.* New York: Teachers College Press.

Perez, William. 2009. *We Are Americans: Undocumented Students Pursuing the American Dream.* Sterling, VA: Stylus.

Reeves, Terrance, and Claudette Bennett. 2003. "The Asian and Pacific Islander Population in the United States: March 2002." US Census Bureau. *Current Population Reports*: 20–540. http://www.census.gov/prod/2003pubs/p20-540.pdf.

UCOP Student Financial Support. 2010. "Annual Report on AB 540 Tuition Exemptions 2008–09 Academic Year." http://www.ucop.edu/sas/sfs/docs/ab540_annualrpt_2010.pdf.

Valenzuela Jr., Abel, and Kevin Escudero. 2009. "California Dreaming: Estimates of Los Angeles DREAM-Act-Eligible Students." Pat Brown Institute of Public Affairs. *Los Angeles 2009 State of the City Report*: 9–13. http://www.patbrowninstitute.org/documents/09SOC_Report_Final_000.pdf.

voices of undocumented students fighting for an education

Edna Monroy, Magali Sanchez-Hall, Natalie Sheckter, and Laura E. Enriquez

I have to be careful . . . because I am [always] worrying that my status [is] going to pop out. Every problem [involves] immigration status.

—Harry Kim, interviewee

Undocumented students wage a constant battle to continue their educations. Whether in community colleges or at four-year universities, these students' immigration status heavily influences the financial resources available to them and their ability to fulfill their higher education aspirations. The passage of California Assembly Bill 540 (AB 540) in 2001 provided some relief to undocumented students by enabling them to pay in-state tuition, significantly lowering the cost of public higher education. Similar policies exist in about ten other states and have significantly increased the number of undocumented students attending college (Flores 2010).

The interviewees for this research study indicated that undocumented students face major obstacles, even with in-state tuition, because they are denied financial aid and barred from legal employment. In only three states, Texas, New Mexico, and most recently California, is financial aid offered to everyone regardless of documentation status (Gonzales 2007). If students manage to overcome these barriers and complete college, their degrees do not lead to employment if they do not have social security numbers. In spite of these limitations, undocumented students have been persevering in school, earning good grades, and becoming active participants in policy debates regarding immigration (Perez et al 2009; Perry 2006). Passing the federal DREAM Act and other local and state policies would increase immigrant student access to public colleges and support the success and contributions of undocumented young adults.

Drawing from thirty-one interviews, we examined the educational experiences of undocumented students. To protect their confidentiality, participants' names have been changed and personal information has been obscured.

Courtesy of Trail of Dreams.

"Without AB 540, I Couldn't Go at All": Undocumented Students' Precollege Experience

One of the biggest sources of undocumented students' motivation is their families. Undocumented students may not have access to financial resources, but most do receive emotional support from their families, contradicting the stereotype that undocumented immigrants do not prioritize or value education. Almost all the interviewees stated that their parents pushed them to continue on to college or were helping them through school financially. Antonia Gonzalez states, "I think my parents had a good effect on me. My dad told me to study and continue studying, because 'that's the only way you're going to be okay when you grow up.' He would always remind me by saying, 'I don't want you being a toilet cleaner when you grow up.'" Hannah Kim, another interviewee, discussed her educational aspirations: "My family was supportive. They knew that we were undocumented, and they said that we have to work twice as hard as other people because we had a higher disadvantage." In both cases, the families have been the most important motivating force for these students.

Resources for undocumented students are sparse, limiting access to higher education. Access to information is also a problem. In California, many undocumented students say that their high-school counselors did not know much or anything about AB 540. Esperanza Vargas recalls a negative experience dealing with her counselor: "My sister was the one who was teaching the counselor about AB 540." Luckily, high schools with large immigrant populations tend to have more knowledge and information on resources like AB 540. Antonia explains that her counselor knew about the legislation but "just told me to go fill out this one form that proved residency, so I just filled it out and didn't ask any questions. . . . I thought that getting a high GPA and good grades was all [I needed] to get financial aid money."

Courtesy of Adrian Gonzalez.

Many undocumented students view higher education as inaccessible because of the costs; however, when students learn about AB 540, their opinions change. Hannah said, "Without AB 540, I couldn't go at all. There was no way I could cover [out-of-state tuition at] $11,000 per quarter. Just tuition alone is $33,000 [per year]. I don't have that much money. If it wasn't for [AB 540], I would still be at a community college. It helped me, and I am very thankful for that."

The Continuous Struggle of Undocumented Students on Their Paths to Higher Education

Although AB 540 allows undocumented students to attend public colleges without paying out-of-state tuition, students encounter other difficulties while attending school. The adversities include economic hardships, instability, and uncertainty about the future.

Employment insecurity is a major challenge that many undocumented young adults must confront. The majority of undocumented students find themselves trapped in low-skilled, underpaid jobs, as they scramble to earn enough money for their tuition. Forced to take any jobs they can find, they work in restaurants and factories and as babysitters, tutors, gardeners, housing, they must commute from home. Because most lack driver's licenses, their commute is by public transportation. Zeus Yun states, "Because I don't have any financial aid, I have to stay off campus; I have to [commute] two hours to campus

My life is a **never-ending struggle**

and housekeepers. Rocio Bañuelos reflects on her experience working arduously to attend school: "I was selling balloons for some time, then I started as a dishwasher at a restaurant. . . . I worked at [a] bakery [as] a cashier. [At my current job, I sell] margaritas, I sell tostadas, [and] take the orders." Sylvia Muñoz describes the unfair labor practices she experienced at a garment factory: "Mostly all the people [that] are undocumented [get paid] cash . . . [and] sometimes they don't pay us. . . . It's worse when it's really hot, and people are sweating . . . people are in need [and they stay] there from sunrise to sundown [with no breaks]." Many undocumented students hold risky jobs in unsafe environments to fund their education.

Access to financial resources has a direct bearing on educational options. Although many of our respondents were accepted into four-year universities after high school, most attended community colleges because of cost. Rosario Torres was accepted at UCLA during her senior year in high school. She describes the joy she shared with her dad: "He was happy and worried at the same time; he knew that I wanted to go there and realized how much it was going to cost him, so I was happy and crying at the same time." Rosario instead attended community college and transferred within three years.

Financial limitations also interrupt students' education. Several interviewees commute up to eight hours a day to school and work. Unable to afford campus

and back. I didn't have a lot [of] options for scholarships."

Many undocumented students work to support not only themselves but also their families. Rocio said, "I live with my dad and my two brothers, so I'm responsible for my two brothers. One is eleven; the other one is fourteen. I go to school full time, taking sixteen units. I get home and do my homework, clean the house. On weekends I work at a restaurant [and] at school, I'm an active student [and] organize events for my club." Commuting, working, family responsibilities, and school work are all part of the daily routine of undocumented students.

This balancing act takes a toll. Rocio shares, "Sometimes I feel depressed. There are so many things against you. But mentally you grow a lot. I think that you become a better person because you have been through a lot of stuff; the future is going to be a lot easier."

Uncertain Futures and Deferred Dreams: After College

When undocumented students graduate from college, their challenges are not over. Jennifer O'Campo explains that she and other undocumented students would benefit tremendously if the DREAM Act were implemented. She feels that it would allow undocumented students "to continue living for our dreams and for our goals, while helping the community . . . . It seems like people have to work around barriers to their goals." Jennifer's frustrations are not unique. Others in similar situations spend most of their time vying for resources to help them finish college. As Jennifer points out, this leaves very little time to think about and plan for life after college. Amanda Su says of her uncertain future after graduation, "If I hadn't been undocumented, I wouldn't have all these uncertainties about the future and what I'm going to do after I graduate, if I go back to school, and where." While other students make plans to travel, apply for jobs, or continue their education, undocumented students have limited options.

Most undocumented students want to become professionals who can contribute to the economy and play constructive roles in their communities. This is evident in Harry Kim's response: "If I had legal status, I would most likely pursue a medical career in graduate school and hopefully have a job in the medical field." Other students explain that they want to be lawyers, computer engineers, business administrators, or doctors.

Adrian Perez states, "I don't want to be too positive or optimistic [in case] something happens like deportation . . . . I don't really want to look onto the future because that is what worries me the most. When you look at a future that you know nothing about, you become more and more desperate about the immediate results that you cannot see." Adrian and others students continue to hope for legislation that will give them the right to use their degrees, such as the DREAM Act or comprehensive immigration reform. In the meantime, undocumented students continue to place their dreams on hold.

Conclusion

Undocumented students are not able to live "normal" lives like the rest of their peers. They worry constantly about their uncertain futures and financial burdens. As Zeus concludes, "My life is a never-ending struggle." Undocumented students fight against all odds to reach for their dreams. Many feel stuck in a broken immigration system. Policies like AB 540 have helped encourage a new generation of undocumented college students but in order to attend college, these students must work several jobs and commute long distances. As graduation approaches, undocumented students increasingly feel a sense of uncertainty and instability. Legislation like the federal DREAM Act would alleviate some of the burdens that undocumented youth face from day to day and would allow them to accomplish their goals and dreams for themselves and their communities. Sylvia explains, "It will not just benefit me, but my whole family, because I will be able to help them out [when I'm] in a better job."

References

Flores, Stella M. 2010. "State Dream Acts: The Effect of In-State Resident Tuition Policies and Undocumented Latino Students." *The Review of Higher Education* 33(2): 239–283. doi: 10.1353/rhe.0.0134.

Gonzales, Roberto G. 2007. "Wasted Talent and Broken Dreams: The Lost Potential of Undocumented Students." Immigration Policy Center. http://www.immigrationpolicy.org/special-reports/wasted-talent-and-broken-dreams-lost-potential-undocumented-students.

Perez, William, Roberta Espinoza, Karina Ramos, Heidi M. Coronado, and Richard Cortes. 2009. "Academic Resilience among Undocumented Latino Students." *Hispanic Journal of Behavioral Sciences* 31(2): 149–181. doi: 10.1177/0739986309333020.

Perry, Andre M. 2006. "Toward a Theoretical Framework for Membership: The Case of Undocumented Immigrants and Financial Aid for Postsecondary Education." *The Review of Higher Education* 30(1): 21–40. http://muse.jhu.edu/journals/review_of_higher_education/v030/30.1perry.html.

graduates reaching a dream deferred (gradd)

Nancy Guarneros, Citlalli Chavez, and Carlos Amador

In loving memory of Tam Tran and Cinthya Felix.

Tam Tran used to joke that perhaps if she were to get a PhD in American civilization, she would then be considered an American. As undocumented immigrant youth in this country, we are raised with the American values of hard work, responsibility, and self-determination. These are the reasons why we continue to fight for an education in an attempt to pursue our dreams. More and more undocumented students are excelling in higher education and receiving bachelor's degrees in a diverse number of fields, and at the same time, taking the reins of our future through the power of a growing social movement for immigrant rights. In both the classroom and the streets, we are creating knowledge and gaining the tools to build a more just society.

One such tool is furthering our education by pursuing graduate and professional academic programs. This is a difficult path, as the graduate application process presents undocumented students with questions and obstacles that may differ greatly from those we faced during our undergraduate studies. Furthermore, with very limited access to graduate funding opportunities, the prospect of attending and completing graduate school can be very challenging, particularly because there continues to be no path toward legalization for undocumented immigrants in this country.

Tam Tran and Cinthya Felix, two undocumented students who were pioneer navigators of the graduate school experience, inspired many other undocumented students across the nation to follow in their path. Tam was a doctoral student in American civilization at Brown University, and Cinthya was at Columbia University

GRADD hosts an educational event for undocumented students interested in pursuing graduate degrees. *Courtesy of Pocho1.*

pursuing her master's degree in public health. On several occasions during their summer breaks, Tam and Cinthya returned to California and spoke on panels where they shared their experiences as undocumented graduate students with groups of future undocumented graduate school applicants. Tam and Cinthya tragically passed away in the midst of their graduate school educations, but their spirit lives on in the work we do now. Graduates Reaching a Dream Deferred (GRADD) is an organization dedicated to providing education and resources for prospective and current undocumented graduate students, to continue the legacy of Tam and Cinthya.

GRADD founding members envisioned the creation of a close-knit undocumented graduate student community that creates a space not only for sharing information and resources but also for establishing lifelong friendships among current and prospective graduate students. The organization hopes that these friendships will lead to a more collective approach to graduate education and future academic and professional goals. GRADD members continue to hear the stories of undocumented students who are succeeding in postgraduate education across the country. From Washington, DC, to Chicago, Illinois, to Cambridge, Massachusetts, students are excelling in graduate education and opening doors for the next generation of undocumented student scholars and professionals.

As more undocumented students pursue graduate degrees, GRADD hopes to promote the academic research the students initiated. These young scholars provide a critical perspective that is greatly needed in immigration literature. Among other topics, graduate students have focused on the undocumented student experience, the influence of visual art in the undocumented student movement, and the intersection of personal identities within the undocumented student population. Additionally our voices are making their way through other fields of study where we are conducting important research in various disciplines.

Through GRADD, we hope to provide an undocumented graduate student narrative for the larger immigration debate. While we continue to be activists, we are also continuing with our graduate studies on campuses throughout the nation. We are emerging as professionals in our fields, but we are pushed into the shadows by the threat of deportation as a consequence of our broken immigration system. We are compelled by a sense of urgency to demand justice for undocumented students and youth, so that we may contribute fully to our communities.

We are **emerging** as professionals in our fields, but we are **pushed into the shadows** by the threat of deportation as a consequence of our **broken immigration system**

Logo design by Raymundo M. Hernández-López, MA (ARYER).

california dream act victory

California Assemblymember Gil Cedillo

California Governor Jerry Brown has given hope and opportunity to thousands of current and future students and their families by signing the California Dream Act, Assembly Bills 130 and 131. The signing of the California Dream Act sends a message across the country that California is prepared to lead the nation with a positive and productive vision for how we approach challenging issues related to immigration.

Ana and Maria Gomez, Jaime Kim, David Cho, Pedro Ramirez, and thousands of other students who are some of the best and brightest in California have been told by our governor and legislative leaders that they are welcome here, that they have something to contribute, that they can be proud of what they have accomplished, and that their talents and ambitions will not go to waste.

The passage of the California Dream Act did not come without struggle. It emerged out of the desire for opportunity and inclusion, but it was initially stymied and vetoed out of an impulse of political fear. The lesson that we learn today is that fear is not an adequate or noble basis for our political aspirations.

The thousands of people and dozens of organizations who continued to fight for the California Dream Act year after year, in spite of the advice of experts and pundits who said it couldn't or shouldn't be done, have now seen their work vindicated. I thank all of them for their continued support through the years. I especially want to thank the students who have worked with my office and staff—students who knew all along that the Dream Act would not be passed in time to help them, but they continued making

California Assemblymember Gil Cedillo, *right*, discusses the California Dream Act with a student. *Courtesy of Pocho1.*